Traveling without Reservations

Traveling without Reservations

THE KIDS GREW UP, THE DOG DIED, WE TOOK OFF!

JEAN GERBER

TRAVELING WITHOUT RESERVATIONS
THE KIDS GREW UP, THE DOG DIED, WE TOOK OFF!

iUniverse books may be ordered through booksellers or by contacting:

iUniverse
1663 Liberty Drive
Bloomington, IN 47403
www.iuniverse.com
1-800-Authors (1-800-288-4677)

Because of the dynamic nature of the Internet, any web addresses or links contained in this book may have changed since publication and may no longer be valid. The views expressed in this work are solely those of the author and do not necessarily reflect the views of the publisher, and the publisher hereby disclaims any responsibility for them.

Any people depicted in stock imagery provided by Thinkstock are models, and such images are being used for illustrative purposes only. Certain stock imagery © Thinkstock.

ISBN: 978-1-4917-8395-5 (sc)
ISBN: 978-1-4917-8397-9 (hc)
ISBN: 978-1-4917-8396-2 (e)

Print information available on the last page.

iUniverse rev. date: 03/03/2016

Contents

CHAPTER 1

Greece

The definition of adventure is to accept the uncertainty, accept the anxiety, accept the doubts, prepare as well as you can, and jump. It is a metaphor for life.

—Bertrand Piccard, renowned hot air balloonist

While we're jammed in our airplane seats en route to Athens, Greece, the captain announces that we are flying over the Atlas Mountains. I don't even know where the Atlas Mountains are! My stomach starts knotting up. This all seemed like a good idea, but what if I hate traveling, get deathly ill, miss the kids, and want to go back? Leaning over Michael to peer down at the mountains reaching up to us through the clouds, I am entranced by their power and beauty. We continue flying, passing over the Mediterranean Sea. I feel a smile come into my cheeks, and the stomach pangs subside.

I remember the day when Michael laid a postcard on the table, ignoring the stack of bills to be paid. "Hey, babe, how about if we sell our house, quit our jobs, and live abroad for a while?"

"Are you kidding me?" I looked at him, trying to figure out if this was serious or just wishful thinking.

"What have we got to lose?" Michael asked. "We can always find work and make money again. We're still healthy and fit, but who knows for how long?"

I looked at the postcard. It said, "We specialize in selling Old Spanish homes in the Coral Gables area and have a client who is interested in buying your house. Would you consider selling it?"

My heart started beating fast. My brain tried to wrap around the idea. I began to imagine the possibility of actually doing this. Though

I had taken a few trips abroad, it was never for any length of time. I felt light-headed and giddy just thinking about it. Our three kids were grown, and they had left the nest. Michael's parents were in reasonably stable health. Mitzi, our beloved miniature dachshund, had passed away the prior summer after fifteen years of providing us with endless love and laughs.

When our house sold, liberating us from the last vestige of suburban life, we were free. Our worldly possessions went into storage. We quit our jobs—much to the amazement, consternation, and thinly veiled jealousy of our coworkers.

"*What!* You are just taking off? How can you do that?"

What excitement to be in control of our lives and to create our own destiny! We are unchained. No keys—not one! Our method of traveling will be "vertical," finding inexpensive pensions or apartments to use as bases from which to explore. We have no interest in counting destinations. Our plan is to stay in each place long enough to get the feel of it, gain an understanding of the culture, and research the possibility of returning permanently one day. We're setting no time limits, no preconceived itinerary, and no reservations.

The Greek Isles is our choice for the first home base, since it's comparatively warm at this time of year, the end of February. Only two weeks prior to our flight to Athens, Michael had a phone conversation with a business acquaintance, an attorney living in Washington, DC. When Michael told him we were going to Greece, he said, "I have a house in the Greek Isles, on Paros. Why not stay there?"

Now here we are, landing in Athens. I am greatly relieved that our luggage arrived. Packing for a trip with no end in sight was a bit of a challenge. I wanted to make sure that I didn't get stuck in some godforsaken part of the world without the most basic essentials— moisturizing shampoo, SPF#50 sunscreen, and guaranteed-to-stay-young skin cream. We also packed our hiking boots, Gore-Tex jackets, and a few clothes, managing to limit our suitcases to one medium and one small each.

The air pollution is the first thing we notice in the city—stifling acrid smog that hangs over us. As we walk higher on the hills, the air becomes more tolerable. We read our *Lonely Planet* and choose an inexpensive hotel that has a view of the Acropolis. We are so tired it doesn't matter that the beds feel like cement slabs. I am anxious to see if my laptop will really work in this part of the world. After several calls to AOL tech support, we are successful. My anxiety about staying in touch with our family lifts.

We start the next morning with Greek coffee. I make the mistake of stirring it, and the coffee grounds come to the top of the cup. I don't want to admit to my ignorance, so I continue to drink it, using my teeth to siphon the grounds. With that, we are sufficiently caffeinated and ready to see the sights of Athens.

Of course, we begin with the touristy sights and start climbing the marble stairs that wrap around the mountain to reach the Acropolis, the Parthenon, and the Temple of Athena. From the top, we have a panorama of Athens. We marvel at how the homes are set into the mountainsides, white structures with painted doors (mostly dark blue) contrasting against dark-brown mountains. Athens was founded in 700 BC. It is fascinating to see the ancient stone homes mixed right in with renovated houses, tiny alleyways running in every direction, old churches on every street, and bearded priests walking purposefully, their long black robes flowing. One can easily imagine this scene 2,000 years ago, unchanged but for the presence of automobiles. Stray cats and dogs navigate the streets like seasoned Manhattan cab drivers.

The following day, we hike up the back of the Acropolis on a steep, well-worn marble path. Perched on a flat rock on top, we watch other people negotiating the same route without the benefit of New Balance sneakers. Their flimsy leather-soled shoes make it a real challenge, but these tourists are determined. At the risk of sliding off the mountain and being buried in rubble, they too make the pilgrimage to the site where so many have previously sat, perhaps listening to the teachings of Socrates.

Next we stumble into our first Greek tavern. Greek *tavernas* are small, cozy restaurants, once you face the fact that everyone inside smokes like a chimney. The food is fresh and good, and cheap. One of our regular meals consists of fresh grilled fish, steamed vegetables, Greek salad, and a piece of baklava for dessert.

"Good morning" (*kalimera*) and "thank you" (*efharistó poli*) are all we know in Greek, but three days later, we add three new words. At this rate, in about six months I should be able to say, "I am hopelessly lost, have no drachmas, need to use the bathroom, and am about to burst into tears. Can you please help me?"

The Plaka is an old historical neighborhood clustered around the slopes of the Acropolis, with labyrinthine streets and neoclassical architecture. It is filled with restaurants, touristy gift shops, and an abundance of *souvlaki* stands. This classic Greek street food consists of small chunks of meat and veggies grilled on a skewer. We can't get enough, eating it every chance we get. There is even an organ grinder (*sans* monkey) wheeling his decorative wooden apparatus around the narrow streets, smiling, posing for my camera. The alleys are crowded with tiny foreign cars belching fumes. The motorbikes are even worse. How can people drive on these narrow, twisting streets and straight-up hills? We actually see a taxi driving down a flight of stairs. We are the only ones who seem to think these terrifying techniques are out of the ordinary. The Plaka's streets and sidewalks are made of marble, even the curbs. It's not unusual to come across an archaeological dig of an ancient burial ground or part of an ancient city or monastery, which the kids use for playgrounds.

The folks we encounter are amicable, and many speak some English, although simple things can still be a challenge. We have to get in line three times at the post office to mail a small package: one line to buy the box, a second line for tape and string, and the last line for postage. Our hotel room phone doesn't work, so we walk down the hill, find the nearest pay phone, buy a phone card, and manage to make a call. The next challenge is finding our way back to the hotel. Michael has a better sense of direction in Athens than in Miami, but that isn't saying much as he admits to being directionally challenged. But he finds the hotel, another small victory.

What a joy just walking and looking at the stores, buildings, and people. I feel excited to be in another part of the world, trying different foods, hearing a strange language, not knowing what awaits me around the corner. My senses are awakened; my eyes are wide open. I am alive. Perhaps this is what it means to live in the moment.

I squeeze Michael's hand, happy to send this energy into him and share it.

Ready to roll, Miami

Here we are in Athens

The streets of Athens

CHAPTER 2

Paros, Greece, in Winter

Traveling out of season has several compensations other than a cheaper ticket. There is, for instance, a certain smug and unworthy satisfaction in traveling against the flow.

—Peter Mayle

We arrange our flight from Athens to the island of Paros for March 1. It's about a half-hour ride on a small (perhaps twenty-seat) fast propjet. The view from the plane flying into Paros clearly shows the little island, with its lagoons reflecting the blue sky and brown and green mountains adding texture to the terrain. It reminds me of a children's board game; I believe it is Candy Land. The whitewashed homes are clustered near the shores of the island and thin out as the mountains get steeper.

The flight lands smoothly, and we call Demetrius, the manager of the Sunset Hotel, and the caretaker of the home of our Miami acquaintance. Demetrius speaks only a word or two of English, but he is expecting us. Our taxi arrives at his hotel. We introduce ourselves and jump into his little truck. The house is located about five minutes from the center of Paroikia, the main city of Paros. At long last, we will see our future (albeit temporary) abode. As we head up and around the final stretch, a straight shot up a rocky road, I look back over my shoulder and take in the most magnificent view: the green fields of the mountain, a church steeple, the Aegean Sea, and the ferry boats approaching the port culminating in luminescent colors of green, blue, and white.

The dwelling is a centuries-old farmhouse that was renovated about a year ago. The road runs above the house, and to get into the house you walk down a steep path that leads to the back and then down and around to the front, which faces out toward the sea. White stucco interior and exterior walls support bamboo ceilings with wooden beams. The house has several entrance doors and shuttered windows. It's roomy, but not huge. A primitive kitchen with a two-burner propane tank gas stove and a sink area with a marble counter await my cooking endeavors. The view out the window is serene, and I gaze over the field immediately in front of us, beyond the little house below and out to the velvety blue sea sparkling in the sun. I don't mind the small refrigerator or lack of cabinets or shelves; it just means we cannot go berserk at the supermarket. We plan one day's meal at a time. The layout maintains the floor plan of the original farmhouse, but the walls have been rebuilt, and the floor throughout is polished flagstone. Nooks in the walls hold candles and books. The original cooking fireplace remains in the kitchen area, and although it's not in use anymore, it adds to the charm of the place. A complete and relatively modern bathroom with a tub/shower combination, toilet and sink, and a washing machine puts us at ease. There is a window for ventilation and light. A stone fireplace in the wall of the living room and a cozy built-in seating area will keep us warm on cool evenings. One step up and through a door, I enter the bedroom, with its double doors opening onto the deck facing a large mountain (complete with a herd of grazing goats). A second small bedroom with a fireplace can be found up a step off the master bedroom.

Despite having very little furniture, it's sufficient—a beautiful wrought iron bed, a wooden chest, and a little bistro table and chairs we can set up outside (when the weather permits) for our meals. Two huge Greek urns and a couple of Turkish rugs add a nice touch; we've stumbled into the perfect place to start our adventure.

The house has been closed up for nearly a year. It's damp and cold. *Really* cold. As soon as Demetrius drops us off, we look at each other.

"This place is great."

"Really great."

"Uh-huh."

"Now … where can we buy a space heater?"

We have no car, so we head back down the mountain to the stores that Demetrius pointed out to us. It's a twenty-minute walk down the hill to the road that appears to be the main drag. We find a general store and begin the challenge of trying to explain that we want to buy an electric heater. Evidently, "heater" in English must sound like "cooking pot" in Greek because that's what the clerks keep showing us. Lo and behold, behind the pots we spot a heater. A couple of blocks farther, we see linens in a store window and purchase a heavy fleece blanket that costs about US$40. The saleslady keeps trying to sell us a cheaper one, but we won't let her take the fleece out of our hands. We stop in the market, stock up on *ouzo* (the standard local intoxicant) and a couple of other emergency items, throw as much as we can in the backpacks, and carry the rest in our arms, heading back up the mountain. The hike warms us, and with our newly purchased space heater and blanket, we make it through our first night snug as can be.

* * *

The next day we wake to the sounds of cowbells, mooing, and roosters crowing. I look out the door and see a scene right out of *The Sound of Music*. Our neighbor, whom we have since learned is named Yurgi, is shepherding his flock of sheep and goats with the help of two dogs in the field behind our farmhouse. I wave, grab my camera, and take several pictures. He tolerates me quite well, better than his sheep, which steer clear of the photographer. Yurgi and I stare at each other for a few minutes—I tell Michael he looks just like Anthony Quinn in *Zorba the Greek*. Yurgi asks a question and I say, "No problem." I hope he was asking if it is okay to let his animals graze in the field by our house, but I am not really sure what I'm actually agreeing to.

"By the way," Michael explains, "Anthony Quinn is Mexican. His real name is Antonio Reyna, which means 'queen' in Spanish, *ergo* Anthony Quinn!" Michael often entertains me with his trivia.

Demetrius picks us up the next day and drops us off at the car rental place owned by his cousin. Michael cuts a deal for a Suzuki four-wheel drive Jeep-type vehicle.

"Should we lock the doors?" Michael asks the agent.

"Yes. You have to be careful of the Albanians."

"Oh," we respond, puzzled.

I have to refer to our map of the world to locate where Albania is in relation to Greece. I guess every country has its share of immigrants hoping for a better life, and there are naturally a number of shady characters among them, not to mention the historical ethnic rivalries that are common to the human lot.

The days are clear, breezy in the hills, and the weather warms up deliciously as morning progresses into afternoon, reaching the upper sixties. We have no television and have only read one newspaper since we've been here, so we guess at the temperature. The hot sun works wonders to force the night chill out of our bones. Evenings are clear and cold, maybe in the low fifties, which is cold as far as I'm concerned. The first three nights we have a full moon that lights up the road and makes for a very pleasant walk down the mountain to a sweet little bakery that seems always to be open.

Eager to connect the phone in our farmhouse so that we can be in touch with our family and monitor our financial status, we make several visits to the office of the electric company. An electrician finally comes over to check out the phone line to see if they can get it working. He makes a call on his cell phone and then mumbles something to us about coming back later. A couple of weeks pass, and the electrician returns. We watch as he constructs a ladder out of various scraps that he finds in the field in order to reach the top of the telephone pole and make the necessary connections. Finally, we are online and in touch.

Happy to have our connections set up, we settle into a routine. We set up breakfast each morning outside on the north patio, right off the bedroom. They have sweet, juicy, seedless, locally grown oranges here in Paros. We have several lemon trees on our property as well. The eggs are fresh and sold individually in the little local grocery store, so you need an egg carrier to transport them. The yogurt is creamy and rich, and we top it off with locally produced honey, bananas, and pure fruit juices, which are addictive.

We open up all windows and doors while we're home during the day, and our farmhouse begins to dry out a little. Although we haven't run into any Albanians, Yurgi's goats pay us visits. Michael nearly has a heart attack when he wakes from his nap and finds himself face-to-face with the bravest of the tribe, who walks right through the bedroom doors as if he owns the place.

Most mornings after breakfast we venture into the center of town. The high season doesn't start up until Easter, so many of the hotels and restaurants are closed. The local enterprises are busy finishing new construction and putting fresh coats of whitewash on their buildings in anticipation of the hordes of tourists and part-time residents. It's nice now because there are no crowds, just the locals, but I confess that I am also looking forward to high season, when more places will be open.

At sunset one afternoon, we decide to explore a bit. We drive our jeep north to the village of Naoussa. It's a ten-minute drive through agricultural fields and along a winding road that overlooks the sea. The coastline is magnificent—huge cliffs descend right into the sea, and gentle lagoons weave in and around them. The sand is the color of light-brown sugar, made of tiny stones instead of shells. The water is very cold, but clear. How wonderful it will be when it warms up enough for a dip. Once in Naoussa, we park at a harbor where there are dozens of colorful fishing boats and Greek fishermen standing around in groups discussing the day's catch. We discover several little restaurants, but we'll have to wait until they open for the season.

Walking around, we come across a church in the center of town that holds Friday night services, and we're drawn to it by the mesmerizing voice of the cantor. The doors are open, so we're able to get a glimpse of the service in progress. The congregation is mainly comprised of women dressed in dark skirts and black stockings, and most have black scarves on their heads. We are moved (and perhaps slightly depressed) by the solemnity of the service.

Up the street is a little restaurant that serves *gyros* (pronounced "yeros"). The waiter brings us each a platter of delectable roasted pork, sliced so that each piece has a bit of crunchy crust and tender, flavorful meat. This is tossed with cooked red onions and accompanied by a yogurt-dill sauce, tomatoes, and French fries, which are evidently served with every meal in Greece. Afterward, we check out the local pharmacy for Tums, just in case, and are pleased to learn that indeed they do sell them (and most of the other stuff I schlepped from Miami—who knew?).

Since we are living here in Paros, we have to do our everyday chores, like laundry. Our house has a washing machine, but dryers are not part of the culture, judging by the fact that every household hangs its laundry outside for the entire world to see.

Michael says, "Don't worry, skid marks are *de rigueur.*"

There is plenty of hot water and a large bathtub into which I dump in about three cups of water softener—the water is hard on the skin and hair, but otherwise fine. It leaves me thinking about one of our walks into town, where I passed a real, honest-to-goodness spa that offers glorious treatments for face and body. I may live in the country, but I don't want to look like one of Yurgi's goats.

* * *

One evening, we stop at Pebbles, a charming bistro run by a Scottish lady named Karen. She provides colorful insights into the quality of the restaurants on the island. We take her advice and have dinner at a Japanese/Chinese restaurant called Norio's. They serve a wide variety of Asian cuisine, but no raw fish.

Karen says, "Our clientele has not yet developed a taste for it."

The chef sits with us for a while, then Karen joins us with a friend, and soon we're all having fun. Best of all, the waiter, a young Greek man named Makis, whose English is quite good, makes it his mission to teach us a few Greek expressions to help us get by. We make a date for a lesson tomorrow. So, good food, good company, and Greek lessons—you can't beat that!

Today we have a wonderful meal of fried calamari and grilled octopus at a traditional Greek restaurant owned by a lady from Brussels. How delightful it is to sit outside by the waterfront, gazing at a glorious sunset and eating a scrumptious dinner.

The weather since we arrived in Paros has been very consistent. The days start out sunny and cool, with just the hint of a breeze, and then the wind picks up as the afternoon approaches. Accordingly, we shift our chairs outside to catch the warm rays and stay out of the chilly breeze. Down in the village it's much warmer, so we have been frequenting the *tavernas* for coffee and conversation with the shop owners and acquaintances. Every day we do at least one good hike up and down the mountains, and our legs are getting strong and muscular.

While in town, we meet a young man in his late twenties from Oregon who is here to prepare his father's apartment for the high season ahead. Kevin has traveled quite a bit, and he's delightful company. He visits us at the farmhouse, and he and I set out to climb the mountain facing our home, which I have wanted to do ever since I arrived. It takes an hour and several briars in our butts to get to the top, but the view of the Aegean Sea and the surrounding mountains is well worth the effort. There are some shelters made of stone at various places high up on the mountain for the shepherds to take refuge from the wind. I marvel at how they have probably been there for centuries, unchanged. The farmers cultivate the ground in terraces, creating a layered effect, using rocks collected from the plowed fields to form inclined buttresses. The fields go way up into the mountains, and the farmers still use donkeys to work them. It is challenging, but I get the feeling that the farmers would not willingly change one thing about their lifestyle. Most of the town's shop owners also own a piece of land on which they raise livestock.

Back at our farmhouse, we've been enjoying visits from a beautiful golden retriever-type dog. The dog looks well cared for, and we have so far resisted the urge to feed him, lest he become dependent on us.

This morning we see "our" friendly dog walking with a tall, handsome blond young man, and we introduce ourselves. Rob is the caretaker of the house directly below ours, is from Vancouver, Canada, and is an English teacher. He has been here since December and will stay until May. We learn that the dog's name is Koita (pronounced "keeta") and that he is, indeed, well cared for. Rob works at a wildlife preserve in Paros and offers to take us there in the morning. The preserve cares for injured wildlife—owls, eagles, ducks, swans, seagulls. Even blind stray cats have found a home there. Greek citizens don't really support the center; it is funded mostly by private donations from foreigners and is staffed by volunteers. Most of the injuries they see are the result of being shot by hunters and farmers, and many injuries are so severe that the creatures can never be set free. However, at certain times of the year, the center organizes a release in northern Greece for the few fortunate ones that can return to the wild.

Today we decide to venture out beyond our little neighborhood and take a long drive. The main road out of town circles the entire island, and it takes about forty-five minutes from beginning to end. The road winds high up into the mountains, allowing us to look down the green hillsides and out at the calm, aquamarine Aegean Sea. It is a spectacularly clear day. In the distance, we can see the shapes of Naxos, Ios, Syros, and some of the other neighboring islands. We stop at an artists' village called Lefkes in the middle of Paros. The village is built into a V-shaped valley with homes and apartments etched up and down the mountain. At the top of one side, we look down onto the rooftops and terraces and up the other side of the mountain at even more apartments and homes. It's all a maze of flagstone alleys graced by whitewashed homes and flowering trees and gardens. At one point in the center of town, we must park our car and walk, as the roads are too steep and narrow to drive. With the backdrop of the mountains and the sea, the result is one of the most charming villages that we have ever seen.

While we walk through Lefkes, we stop to admire a pretty garden with flowers, birdcages, and tables. A gentleman comes out of his home and invites us in for tea and pistachio nuts, which have been harvested from his trees. His name is Sterios Kalamaras; he owned one of most famous Greek restaurants in London. There are dozens of pictures of him with celebrities and articles about his restaurant on his walls. He recommends a couple of restaurants on the island; we're looking forward to trying them.

* * *

It's such a gift to settle into this lifestyle. We enjoy our walks to the little market for locally grown produce: lemons, potatoes, tomatoes, zucchini, cucumbers, and green peppers. We go to our favorite bakery for fresh loaves of crusty sesame-seed bread, and then to the local butcher for fresh chickens. I develop an aversion to eating lamb or veal, since I pass by those little critters every day and have become very fond of them.

I think the mountain air—or maybe the stress-free environment— makes the simplest things seem hysterically funny. For example, Michael decides that it is time to take a shower, which in and of itself demands strong willpower because it is *really* chilly in the morning. He warms the bathroom with our one and only space heater and proceeds to take a long hot shower. Now the sun is shining and the breeze is fresh, and I think it's a good time to air out the place from the previous night's fireplace fiasco. We had tried to warm the house with lousy, damp wood that wouldn't burn, but which did nearly smoke us to death. I proceed to open *all* the doors and windows just as a tremendous shutter-clanging, door-slamming breeze comes whistling through. At that very moment, Michael steps bare-assed out of the bathroom. He can't believe my timing. At the sight of his consternation, I completely lose it and am laughing so hard that the tears roll down my face. I can't look at Michael without returning to my fit of hysterics. He doesn't think it is so funny.

We've become acquainted with several people, and because the island is small, we see one or two of them each time we're out. It feels like home here. Somehow our days are filled, and we look at each other and ask, "How did this day pass by so quickly?" We attempt to attend the one cinema that is open this time of year, which we find on a tiny alley off the main street. A couple of high school boys sit out front, and we ask them if this is, in fact, a movie theater. They confirm that it is and that the movie will start in about half an hour. Both kids speak English, and we have a nice conversation with them. One of the boys spends his summers with his American mother in Texas but has lived on Paros for ten years with his Greek father. It was interesting to hear about island life through the eyes of a teenager. He says he really likes living here because he has close friends, and it's a safe place to be. He says there is no crime. While we are talking, a man comes up and says a few words in Greek to them.

They translate for us. "There's been an accident. The projector is broken, and the movie will now be postponed until Sunday evening."

We never find out what movie is playing, but we'll surely give it another try. The kids work at the theater, and we're looking forward to seeing them again.

Despite all the magic we're experiencing in Greece, the weather suddenly changes for the worse. It's windy, rainy, and cold, with scattered moments of sunshine, but that doesn't keep us from enjoying this gorgeous place. We are layered in the strangest of clothing combinations, but hey, whatever works. *Ouzo* is a helpful remedy, and our comforter is toasty warm, so we've had no problem sleeping. We read books, cook, shop, and explore during the day. We just can't get enough of the beauty on this island.

* * *

The ferryboats that go to the neighboring islands of the Cyclades (Naxos, Santorini, and Mykonos) are easy to book and inexpensive. For example, it's about US$8 per person one-way for a four-hour ferry ride to Santorini. We think that we'll go check it out in a couple of weeks when a few more places open up for the season.

Michael is growing a beard, and he's beautifully bronzed from the sun. I can picture him casting nets off one of those fishing boats docked in the harbor. His name in Greek is *Mikalis*. Mine's a little more complicated, since they don't have a "J" in the Greek alphabet, so it ends up being spelled *Tzhn*—which, believe it or not, sounds like "Jean."

Many of the *tavernas* are run by families, typically with the TV constantly blaring. We eat dinner at one place called To Stecki—where we are becoming regulars—and *Xena: Warrior Princess* is playing tonight with Greek subtitles. There is a huge spit at this place, slowly turning, laden with pork, chicken, and lamb for the *gyros*, and whole chickens roasting over hot coals. The aroma is tantalizing. The wine is bottled right here in Paros—a fruity, light, drinkable blend that accompanies any meal. When we are seated at the table, a piece of thin, disposable plastic or paper is laid over the tablecloth, and then the plates are put down. Silverware and paper napkins are stuffed into a drinking glass and set on the table. It's casual, needless to say, but the food is fresh and tasty. The owners of To Stecki break out their homemade wine. It is cloudier than the bottled stuff, but *wow*, it is good. We make such a fuss over it that they keep refilling our tin cups. I don't remember much after that, but Michael somehow gets us safely home and tucked into bed.

We awake to a day that is cold but clear. We go for our usual hike up the mountain and work up a good sweat, and as the path ends, we find ourselves at the entrance of a small centuries-old stone monastery. We pay our spiritual respects, and as we start heading back down, we find ourselves hot on the trail of a herd of sheep and goats. We return to our wonderful farmhouse for a big breakfast of fresh bread and island-made honey, bananas, kiwi, and an omelet with sweet onions, zucchini, and tomatoes. Not a bad morning!

Demetrius

Farmhouse in the foreground

Yurgi and his flock

What's for breakfast!

Café in town

Rachel visits us

Naoussa

CHAPTER 3

Paros, Spring

The paradox of our time in history is that … we've
learned how to make a living, but not a life; we've added
years to life, not life to years.

—George Carlin

There is one café in particular that seems to draw the expatriates
who live on Paros. Everyone seems to have plenty of time for a cup of
coffee and storytelling. And what a variety of characters! When we
first arrive, we notice a handsome blond man, probably in his thirties,
Rollerblading through town carrying a small dog—no easy feat on
these rough stone streets—trailed by three other dogs. He is something
straight out of Southern California and so out of character for Paros
that I have to snap a couple of pictures as he flies past me. Fortunately,
we run into him at the café. Don is an ex-hockey player from Canada
who divides his time between California and Paros. He *never* takes off
his Rollerblades. He has been living in Paros for four years, working
on sculptures that have been commissioned by his patrons. He invites
us to his studio apartment, and we spend an enjoyable afternoon with
him. His work is beautiful. It has long been his dream to come to Paros
and sculpt with marble from the local quarries. Paros has been famous
throughout history for its pure white marble, from which some of the
world's most famous sculptures have been created, including the Venus
de Milo. He has a simple life—just the bare necessities—and seems
quite content with it. When we meet Don, we gain an even greater
appreciation for the relaxed and wonderful scene in which we find
ourselves. People respond to our interest with complete openness, a
profound experience for us.

21

Meanwhile, Michael has a lively conversation with a Brit from Liverpool, in his early sixties I would guess, who is a carpenter on the island. His adventures have ranged from being a bartender on a cruise line for five years to being in barroom brawls at various locations around the world. He hung around the Beatles in Liverpool just before they were discovered. Later, he made some wise land investments in Canada, and this affords him a lifestyle of his choosing. He has a twinkle in his bright blue eyes, wears a wool stocking cap and an old beat-up sweater, has a nose that's about thirty degrees off-center (from a sucker punch in a bar in Ft. Lauderdale), a chipped front tooth, and an unforgettable grin.

At the same table is a woman named Madeleine, age sixty-three, who has an Australian accent, long brown hair streaked with gray, a tanned face with ruddy cheeks, and startling blue eyes. Originally from Luxembourg, she married an Australian who had a fatal accident here on Paros. Now a widow, she told me that Paros is a place that will either accept you or not. She says that, before he died, her husband had a premonition that the island would defeat him, and she told us to be careful.

We enjoy our Greek acquaintances as well. Pericles, the bartender at Pebbles, is a twenty-five-year-old who speaks English and shares some stories with us over a glass of *ouzo*. His parents live in Athens, as well as his girlfriend. He tells us about his beloved German shepherd, and how the dog was shot by a neighbor. Evidently the neighbor had grown tired of having to divert his flock of sheep away from Pericles's guard dog, so he shot him. Pericles admits that in retaliation for his dog, he shot three of the neighbor's sheep. This must be how wars are started. He refuses to let us pay for our drinks and declares that they are "on him."

When Michael insists on paying, he says, "No. That is not the Greek way. If you were to pay, you would be refusing my gift, and that would be an insult."

How can we argue with that? Especially when we consider the dog-retaliation story. Of course, we are now obligated to a return visit with Pericles and will spend several hours drinking and talking with him. I can think of a lot worse ways than the Greek way.

Then there is Pavlo, who always has the most wonderful smile on his handsome face. He greets us warmly when we come into his store to buy our *International Herald Tribune*. We generally have to wait for the ferry that carries the newspapers to arrive, so there is plenty of time for a chat. Fortunately for us, he speaks some English.

We enjoy reading the *International Herald Tribune*. It arrives in Paros a day late, unless the boats are held up by bad weather. The paper, affiliated with the *Washington Post*, provides a reasonably unbiased view of what's happening in the world. The inside section concerns Greece (we get the English translation), editorials are mostly about Europe, and we even get Dave Barry in the Sunday issue.

✳ ✳ ✳

Michael's parents call us today, concerned about our safety because of the NATO bombings in Kosovo. It is a surprise to me because we feel so safe here; it is infinitely safer than Miami. Lisa, our eldest daughter, e-mails us with the same concern. With her gift for words and humor, she writes:

> I'm worried about you guys. What do the other ex-pats (American and European) that you have met say about the NATO strikes and anti-American rioting? You know all Italian airports are closed for commercial flights. Maybe you guys should move to Israel? I trust you if you think you're safe, but I want regular reassurances (like, every day). You know, something like, "Hi, we're alive, no refugees in the backyard, our neighbors love America, and NATO is more popular than *ouzo*."

A more pressing concern for us is what to have for dinner. Michael goes down the hill to our favorite little family restaurant to buy a chicken for takeout. While he is waiting for the chef to cook it to perfection, the Greek owner brings out his own special brew of *schuma*. It is a new experience for him, and he learns that it is what *real* Greeks drink, to be shared only with friends and family. Michael describes it as a cross between cognac and lighter fluid. One hour later, stumbling back home with a cooked chicken in hand and thoroughly drunk, Michael says, "It sure beats KFC!"

On a more serious note, we gather that everyone is concerned that the United Nations bombings of Kosovo might have a negative effect on the forthcoming Easter festivities and tourist season. A large portion of people's livelihood on Paros is based on the short season, and they fear the incident will alienate the Americans, British, Germans, Italians, and French. The Greek government was not in favor of the UN accord. Serbs and Greeks are followers of the Eastern Orthodox Church and were bound by alliance treaties and co-belligerence in wars since the Middle Ages. The population of Albania and Kosovo is mostly Muslim, and the Greeks feel a strong enmity toward them. The possibility of refugees streaming across the northern border of Greece from Yugoslavia concerns the locals. However, due to Greece's desire for full partnership in the European Union and additional economic reasons, no one can afford to take a stance against NATO's action. The local section of the paper announced a few of the locations in Athens where anti-NATO rallies were being held. There is no American consulate on Paros, so the island seems very far removed from it all.

There's not much we can do to change politics or wars, so we decide to do a little exploring. Antiparos, which literally translated means "opposite Paros," is a fifteen-minute ferry ride and costs US$2 per person one way. We enjoy an afternoon there. The hotels, restaurants, and bars are situated on the main street, a short walk from the pier, but they are shut tight until tourist season. We find one open café that serves only drinks and coffee, but thankfully a little food market is also open. We buy cheese made in Antiparos, which tastes a little like Parmesan, only milder, and is wonderful. We buy freshly baked bread and salami that was made in Crete, cut into quarter-inch slices, and a couple of locally grown oranges. We bring our purchases to the café and have a delicious *frappe* (iced coffee made with whipped cream) and watch the action down at the pier. We are fascinated, and a bit horrified, as we watch a man pounding the hell out of a poor little octopus, smashing it again and again on the cement of the pier. We ask the English-speaking waiter what it is all about, and he assures us that this is the Greek way to tenderize an octopus. Evidently, it must be smashed against the pier a hundred times to properly tenderize it! After our lunch, we walk to the pier, and by this time the man has a whole pile of octopus that he has properly tenderized. He washes them in the sea to remove the ink. We ask if we can take a picture, and he smiles and poses. After we get our shot, he hands the string of octopus to me and indicates that I should have my picture taken while sloshing the octopus in the seawater. So, I do. After being cleaned, they are strung on a clothesline to dry. I have had grilled octopus since this episode, and I can assure you that it is tender and tasty. Still, I can't help but think of the arduous process of smashing and sloshing these poor little creatures.

On Antiparos, we pass by a small school where the kids are outside practicing their parade techniques for the upcoming holiday—Greek Independence Day, March 25. This marks the beginning of the final revolt against the Ottoman Empire in 1821—basically, it's when they threw out the Turks.

Independence Day is celebrated in Paros with a parade that features the marching band from the school, with the children dressed either in school uniform or in colorful Greek costumes. It is a good opportunity to see the parents as well. All the shops and supermarkets close for the holiday, and everyone turns out for the parade. The women dress conservatively—no jeans, and even slacks are rare. The men dress in shirts and sport coats, but again, no jeans for this occasion. Women under thirty are quite stylish and attractive—very pale skin and dark hair. Women over thirty look like they could be anywhere from forty to sixty years of age, perhaps older. Older women must wear mourning clothes for the rest of their lives when there has been a death in the family—in *anyone's* family, from the looks of it. Who knows, maybe even when their goat dies! The horde of women dressed in black looks like a scene from a Greek version of Grimm's fairy tales.

* * *

They say that necessity is the mother of invention, and on an island one gets in the habit of using whatever materials are at hand. Take my hair products, for example—most notably, the Frizz-Ease, which is wonderful for squeaky doors (it preserved our sanity at the hotel in Athens, where the bathroom door sounded like someone was slaughtering a cow). The VO5 hairdressing cream has proven to be particularly effective for removing ticks from Koita, who now spends most of the day with us while Rob is at work. Olive oil serves many purposes—cooking, body moisturizing, hair conditioning, supplementing Koita's food—and it's economical. I've used up the products that I brought with me from the United States and discovered that the natural products are far superior. Of course, Mediterranean women have known this for centuries.

In the past, my kitchen was well stocked. Overstocked, really. Now I work efficiently with two saucepans, one frying pan, a plastic bowl, and a few eating utensils. The same is true with my clothes. I don't need to switch my wardrobe from season to season. I simply add or remove an extra layer when needed. Minimalism is my new mantra. We are eating just as well, we are comfortably clothed, and we have a lot more time to do whatever we wish.

* * *

When a civilization is over 5,000 years old, there are plenty of traditions to pass along. In fact, if the word *traditional* is not in its description, forget about it. The Greeks pride themselves on their *traditional* Greek restaurants, serving *traditional* Greek cooking, *traditional* Greek wine, and so on. In the United States, most restaurants have a variety of ethnic foods on the menu, but in Greece, Greek food is the only item. For the most part it is tasty, nutritious, and satisfying. But I've developed a craving for soup, and the only soup we've seen in Greece is either *traditional* fish soup or *traditional* Greek gigantus bean soup. We had the fish soup in Athens, and it was yummy. We liked the gigantus bean soup well enough (despite the aftereffects), but I'm craving *traditional* Jewish chicken soup. I'll have to do without matzo balls, no doubt.

I buy a chicken at the little supermarket that I have earmarked as "safe for poultry." Actually, it is the only supermarket where I find chicken because everyone on the island seems to raise their own chickens. The butcher reaches under the counter and shows me a large dead chicken. I ask him to please remove all excess body parts—such as feet, feathers, beaks, and eyeballs—before he hands it over to me. I load up on veggies, fresh herbs, and spices and go home to cook. All is simmering along well enough when we run out of propane gas. Michael, bless his heart, knows how much I want chicken soup and insists on going out to get the propane tank refilled.

So, it is eight o'clock in the evening on Good Friday. Logic tells Michael to visit the one gas station in the vicinity, but not surprisingly, it is closed for the holiday. He wonders if the supermarket might have a small propane tank, but when he asks, the manager tells him that they are closing right that minute and claims that if they stay open one minute later, the Greek government will fine the supermarket huge sums of drachmas, throw them both in jail, and serve them nothing but *traditional* Greek gigantis bean soup for the next twenty years. Finally, Michael thinks to ask his friend Pavlos where he can find a refill for the tank. Pavlos has the answer. He directs Michael to an alley behind another alley a little ways off. So, Michael goes on foot with the empty tank on his shoulders. The alleys in town are too narrow for a car and can barely accommodate one five-foot, eleven-inch man carrying a gas tank. He tromps all over the place and eventually figures that he might have a better chance of finding a Bagel Emporium than he would to locate the tank refill place. Eventually he spots a little man carrying a big propane tank, and he follows him to the right place. At ten o'clock, in the dark, Michael lugs the filled tank up the hill and to our home, makes the proper connections without any tools, and we are able to enjoy the most delicious bowl of soup we've ever eaten.

※ ※ ※

Easter arrives. The entire country is Greek Orthodox, so you can imagine the importance of this holiday. Stores close for the week, and everyone takes a rest. After we enjoy the last of our chicken soup, we walk to the church in the center of town to view the Good Friday festivities. The bishop comes out of the church in full regalia, impressive with his snow-white hair and long beard. A group of eight men follow him, carrying a large coffin with the images of Jesus's crucifixion painted on top. The entire population of Paros must have been there, dressed in their Sunday best. It is oppressively quiet and somber.

The Easter celebration that follows the next night is a much happier affair. Everyone brings a candle to the town square just before midnight on Saturday. Eventually, the bishop shows up (he says that he's on "God's time," and evidently God doesn't own a watch). He descends from the church with a lighted candle and ignites someone else's. The flame is then passed on from candle to candle, until the candles of the entire congregation light up the night. After that, it's off to the *tavernas* to begin a twenty-four-hour feast. Michael and I do not join in on this. Instead we go back to our farmhouse and have a private celebration stargazing on our rooftop.

We accept an invitation to join Demetrius and his family and guests for a *traditional* Easter meal. The weather is perfect, and we bring a couple of bottles of wine made in Paros. This turns out to be the next best thing to bringing your own homemade wine, which is what *real* Greeks bring to dinner. We show up around one-thirty in the afternoon, even though the invitation says to come around noon, having learned that Greek time operates very much like Latin time—dinner was just being served. The Easter fare starts with chopped lamb's liver and rice with a sauce that is indescribably awful. We move quickly to the grilled vegetables: eggplant, zucchini, and peppers, which are a lifesaver. They also serve a fresh Greek salad and some fresh bread, and then … the lamb. It is cut into chops. Michael has no qualms about eating them; he and the other guests polish off at least half a herd. Some of the guests are visitors staying at Demetrius's hotel; others are his friends and relatives. At the outset of the dinner, the Greeks speak to each other in quiet voices. There are a couple of Swiss gentlemen with whom we politely converse. After a few liters of wine, though, everyone is able to communicate with each other, and we enjoy some lively conversation.

After recovering from the Easter festivities, we drive our little jeep to the opposite side of the island to a wonderful beach called Piso Livaldi. The international windsurfing championships are held here in the summer, due to the steady breeze from the Aegean Sea and a consistent summer forecast of sunny, clear weather. The beach is composed of brownish grainy sand interspersed with polished pieces of translucent marble. From the shoreline and looking back toward the mountains, you can glimpse the white fractures where the marble is quarried. At last, the day is warm enough to roll up our pants and expose our legs. It is a strange sight, as we haven't seen skin since we arrived! We lay out our picnic of fresh bread, oranges, cheese, and salami—God forbid we should go hungry. Before we know it, two ducks join us. We can't imagine what the ducks are doing along the seashore, but the mystery is solved when we follow them to a stream of fresh water that rushes out of the nearby hills. The brave little ducks proceed to waddle into the sea, paddle out a short distance, and do a little bodysurfing, just for fun. It is most entertaining! Yet again, we both feel so mellow, happy that we are increasingly able to enjoy the simplest things in life, like a raft of ducks goofing off. They apparently work up quite an appetite because they waddle directly up to us to nibble on our bread. After lunch, they swim back up the stream for a well-deserved nap.

Michael and I have heard quite a bit about the Aegean School of Art in the center of town. When we pass by the building, we decide to pop in and check it out. John Pack is the director of the school, and while we are chatting, his wife, Jane, comes in. We hit it off and make plans to have lunch together the next day. In addition to being the director, John teaches advanced photography and has an impressive biography. He came to Paros from New Mexico about fifteen years ago to assume responsibility for the school. Jane and John have been married for ten years, and they have a six-year-old son, Gabriel. Jane, an accomplished painter, also teaches at the school. Her knowledge of the Greek people and the language is remarkable. She is lovely, and I am looking forward to getting to know her better. Gabriel was born in Athens, attends school here, and speaks fluent Greek.

We make a date for the four of us go to lunch at a restaurant called *Thea* (the View). John drives us to the other side of the island, and we end up on a dirt road that leads us to a huge field of chamomile flowers with the restaurant located alongside. The entire front of the restaurant is glass, offering a spectacular view of the Aegean. The bright and cheerful dining room bustles with patrons. John and Jane order several wonderful dishes of *traditional* Greek food (as the restaurant's sign indicates). This lunch renews my faith in Greek cuisine. We start with a shot of *ouzo*, which is served whether you want it or not. It is the restaurant's own distillation, with an alcohol level of ninety-nine percent; its purpose is to increase the appetite and weaken resistance before you order. Once we regain the ability to move our lips, we order appetizers of cooked field greens with subtle lemon and olive oil seasoning, baked feta cheese topped with a spicy red pepper sauce, red beets and yogurt, baked mushrooms stuffed with cheese, and a risotto and mushroom dish. Each one is tastier than the one that precedes it. We are served copious amounts of wine and bread, and then we're brought platters of fresh grilled fish, which has been beautifully filleted, and rabbit with a sweet and spicy prune sauce over wild rice. They serve the dishes family-style, and we continue eating and talking for another three hours.

It isn't long before Nico, the owner, shows up with another jug of homemade liquor. This time it is their finest batch of *schuma*. It would have been an insult not to drink it; we each have a glass. He insists that we toss it down our throats in one shot, as is the custom. Nico serves himself a glass each time that he fills ours and, to be sociable, does this with every table. By the time we are ready to leave, his eyes are as red as the poppies in the field outside. Michael says, "He could be Greece's poster boy for cirrhosis of the liver."

On the way home, John is feeling adventurous and takes the back roads through the mountains. The roads are a bit muddy after the rain that morning and we aren't sure whether his ten-year-old Russian-made car—a Lada—would make it. After a bit of slipping and sliding, we crest a hill and find ourselves in a beautiful meadow resplendent with wildflowers. We stop to pick some purple lupines and listen as the wind carries the sound of goats' bells from the flocks grazing in the distant hills. After such a fantastic meal with wonderful people, the warm glow from the wine, the view from where we stand, a sweet fragrance in the air from the flowers and herbs, and tinkling bells everywhere, I am certain that it simply can't get much better than this.

We become John's art and history students. He points out a thousand-year-old olive tree that still produces fruit. The trunk is huge and gnarly. He obviously loves this place and is a veritable encyclopedia of his adopted homeland. We are tossing questions at him the entire way— about Greek life, the various types of trees, flowers, history, and religion. He is delighted by our enthusiasm and energetically answers everything; we learn so much. We now know that we have fig and almond trees growing next to our house and that the fruit should be ripe in August. Pistachio and apricot trees are blossoming now, and he and Jane point out the wild herbs that grow on the mountain, including oregano, thyme, sage, saffron, and rosemary. By the time they drop us off around five o'clock, I am beginning to think that I could live here forever.

* * *

Koita shows up for his daily breakfast of boiled potato, olive oil, and an occasional scrambled egg. Recently, however, he gives us quite a scare! His face is horribly distorted—his cheeks are puffed out and the underside of his neck hugely swollen. He is drooling and foaming at the mouth, looking quite like a rabid grizzly bear. We alert Rob, who discerns that he has evidently been stung by a swarm of bees or possibly bitten by a snake. Koita is taken to the vet for hydrocortisone shots, and over the next few days the swelling subsides. I don't think he learned his lesson though—I am watching him snap at the air now, trying to catch an insect.

Today, Michael and I set out on what turns out to be a three-hour hike starting at our house. We cross over to one of the mountains facing us and follow a dirt road, which we are told ends at a monastery, as do most of the trails on Paros. The "road" quickly turns into a path with dozens of switchbacks going up and up. We work our way well into the middle of the island and wonder if there really is a monastery or whether that's a myth. Finally we see a white boulder painted with "Poet's Walk" in red letters, with an arrow pointing forward. With renewed hope, we continue on and *up*. It is a challenge, but the flowers are magnificent; the air is scented with wild herbs; the marble glistens in the sun; and the weather is sunny and cool. We expect to spot the monastery at each upward turn. Finally, we spot it across a valley. We rest for a moment, and on the other side of the valley we see a beekeeper dressed in a white robe with a headdress of netting, attending his apiary. It is ethereal, and with the sun low in the sky, everything takes on a warm, golden glow. It feels as though we've entered a secret, magical place, and we follow the path down through the valley and up the other side to the monastery. As we approach this ancient building, we offer a prayer of gratitude. Poet's Walk will stay in my mind for a very long time.

Rachel comes to visit us for a few days, and we enjoy sharing the splendors of Paros with her. She writes to Lisa (her stepsister) the following:

> The P's picked a paradise. From their little farmhouse on the mountain, the views are breathtaking—the Aegean Sea in the distance and the sheep, goats, horses, and cows spot the landscape. Jean and Dad look great, of course. Dad looks very handsome with his beard. Between his dark tan and the salt-and-pepper whiskers, there's no missing the devilish sparkle in his blue eyes, which match the Aegean Sea. And then there's Jean, who seems never to age. She bounds around the mountainside in her sarong and hiking boots, feeding the neglected pups and making friends with all the Greek farmers who don't speak a word of English. I think they're all in love, even the livestock. There's a new Greek goddess in town. Jean is also still cooking

up a storm in the little kitchen. The dishes are as savory as ever. Everything is so fresh: the fruit and veggies, the bread, the fish, and the meats. There's no comparison in the States. I've definitely turned into a glutton over here.

Soon after Rachel leaves, Lisa sends me an e-mail on Mother's Day and includes her Four Top Reasons I Miss My Mother:

Fewer recordings on my machine with messages like, "Hi, honey, just calling to say 'hi' … and to hear your voice … and to find out that everything is okay … and to remind you to get your paperwork taken care of … and to make sure that you bring your car in for servicing … and to say I love you and take care of yourself."
Can't call you to get last-minute cooking instructions.
No one who fully appreciates the depth of excitement when I call to brag about the Most Amazing Pair of Shoes I got on sale.
And the Number One Reason I Miss My Mother is because she is my best friend and I love her!

The kids are managing without us, it appears, although I am always eager to receive e-mail confirmation of this.

Much to our delight, John Pack invites us to join him and his art students on an outing to the oldest and most famous marble quarry on Paros. The white Parian marble from this quarry has been used for many of the world's famous statues, and sculptors from all over the world visit it to pay homage. Michael and I join six students (all girls, as it turns out, much to Michael's delight) on a bus ride to the excavation site. We walk a mile or so until we reach an opening in the mountain and prepare to descend, equipped with flashlights and hiking boots. The descent is quite steep, but we all manage to stay alive. John discusses the quarry's history, pointing out how for thousands of years, slaves carried marble out of this mountain. We descend deeper into the mountain and then sit down together. John asks us turn off our flashlights and to sit quietly for a moment. We obediently follow orders and are instantly swallowed up by the dark stillness of the mine. John turns his flashlight on and shines it through a rock he picked up to show us how translucent the marble is.

We continue down a narrow, steep portion as John points to examples of the finest quality marble in the world. Soon we see the proverbial light at the end of the tunnel, and John asks us to stay put until he summons us. We watch as he climbs up and becomes a tiny silhouette at the front of the opening. The effect of this impressed upon us the almost unimaginable feat it would have been for the laborers to carry huge marble slabs by hand out that deep, dark cave. As we climb, Michael and I don't groan any more or less than the young students. We continue our adventure and hike farther up the mountain to—where else?—a monastery. This ancient building is stark, with open areas within the walls, and the grounds around it are profuse with wildflowers. Some of the few remaining ancient oak trees on the island are found here, and they form a canopy to create a dreamy, absolutely perfect place for a romantic picnic.

John has plans to go to Italy on school business in Pistoia, a short train ride from Florence. He has invited us to come along. The school is situated in a villa donated to the church in the sixteenth century by the Rospigliosi family when one of them was named Pope. The Rospigliosi family still owns fourteen acres of land, on which is a structure that was used to make wine and store lemon trees in the winter. John hopes to someday convert this building into an art and music school with dorms and classrooms. The Rospigliosi family is supportive of this idea; John wants us to come along to show the family that he's gathering supporters. Another couple, Sean and Diana, will be joining us in Pistoia. Students of John's Aegean School of Art attend classes at both locations. Each term, twenty-four students study in Pistoia for a month and then go to Paros for the rest of the semester. He's run the school this way for twelve years and absolutely loves Italy. Besides Pistoia, he can't wait to show us Rome and Florence. How fortunate for us that we will have our friend John Pack to be our personal tour guide.

Everything's traditional!

Don, the Rollerblading sculptor

Michael and Pavlo

First in line for the vet

Our neighbors

Jane and John Pack

CHAPTER 4

Paros, Summer

Do not dwell in the past; do not dream of the future.
Concentrate the mind on the present moment.

—Buddha

After two weeks in Italy on a whirlwind, fantastic visit to Rome, Florence, and Pistoia, we have returned to Paros. This quick overview was just enough to whet our appetites—we plan an extended trip there in the not-too-distant future.

It's the middle of June at 5:30 in the morning and I am awake because the six donkeys grazing on the pasture about a half-mile from our house are braying at their master to come and give them some fresh water. Or perhaps the donkeys have some terrible digestive problems, and that's why they make such a ghastly noise. There is nothing quite comparable to a donkey's *hee-haw*. It begins when the animal fills its lungs with air and lets it all out in one frightfully loud, unearthly bellow, which sounds like the donkey has been stuck in the ass with a hot poker. It lasts no less than three minutes, after which the poor beast is gasping for air—hence the *hee-haw* sound, which goes on for another four minutes or so. This particular sound bounces off the mountains and vibrates the eardrums. Along with this, Koita lets out a mournful, wolf-like howl, which scares the hell out of us, since he is directly under our bedroom window. Our newest household resident, a mouse, is rattling the pans in the kitchen and scurrying around, not at all respectful of our need to sleep and very intent on completing a nest for what might be its future family.

The sunrise bounces off the brown and gold mountains, and its rays blend the colors of the sky with the sea. There has been no rain since May and none expected until October, and the hot sun has baked the fields to a rusty brown. Only the olive and fig trees and grapevines provide some green relief. The wild oleander looks as if splotches of pink paint have been added to the earth tones of the land. The fields of wheat and barley that have not yet been threshed are dry and bleached almost white. When the wind blows through, they rustle softly and sound like raindrops.

It never ceases to delight me to wake up to tinkling goat bells, mooing cows, crowing roosters, barking dogs, and hooting owls. Then there's Antonio, the donkey man, who rides up to his little patch of land every morning around five-thirty and every evening around six to milk and water his two cows, which graze in nearby fields. I assist him one evening, much to my delight (and his, I dare say). I pull about a quarter-cup of milk out of the old gal before she gets thoroughly disgusted with me. Antonio has to finish the job. He speaks a few words of English and is so nice and patient with me. Michael comes over to take a picture, at which point Antonio pulls me very close to him and won't let go. Michael takes more pictures than he actually wants.

June, reputed to be the hottest month, is approaching. We've adopted the Greek schedule: wake up early (there's really no choice in the matter due to the above-mentioned cacophony of critters, the open shutters and windows that let in the cool air, and the glare of the rising sun); do our marketing and errands in town early, to beat the heat; have lunch and a siesta at midafternoon, since it's too hot now for anything more strenuous than that; head to the beach for a long swim; and finally, dinner around nine o'clock in the evening. We read and do our correspondence before bed, and the day is done.

There is no air conditioning, but we haven't felt the need for it. The humidity is low, and we are quite comfortable, as long as we follow the aforementioned schedule. The summer winds blow steadily from the northwest to the southeast on the central and southern Aegean, and in from the Mediterranean coast of Turkey. This wind is called the *meltemi*.

Paros is an incredibly safe haven. There is virtually nothing that can harm you. Well, okay, they supposedly have a poisonous snake called an asp. And then there are Greek drivers, who are infinitely more dangerous than the asp. A favorite Greek pastime is carving notches in the side fenders of their cars (or motorcycles) for every road kill. Foreigners are worth two notches, Greeks are one. Double lines on the highway mean you *must* immediately pass the vehicle in front of you. If you can avoid those deadly creatures, you're sure to live safely and peacefully here.

There is no crime. For example, we have a long-term car rental and are planning to leave town on our Italy jaunt with John Pack. The car rental place is ten minutes from the airport, so we are figuring how we get from one place to the other.

"No problem," says the rental agent. "Just drive the car to the airport, leave it unlocked, and put the keys under the mat."

Wait a second. Did he say to leave the car unlocked with the keys in it? This was a totally foreign concept to us, having lived in Miami for fifteen years.

"It's a small island," he explains, "and everybody knows what belongs to whom."

Another example is when we had a flat tire. Again, we are told, "Don't worry. Leave the keys under the mat, and we'll come and fix the tire. When you get a chance, come to our shop, and we'll give you another car. There's no extra charge for the tire, and we're sorry you were inconvenienced." Imagine Hertz agents telling you this!

I can take a walk—by myself—at any hour of the day or night and never feel threatened by man or beast. No wolves or bobcats hang around. No deadly insects. Even the spiders that come into your home this time of year—which are about five inches in diameter and look like they escaped from a Japanese horror movie—are not at all harmful, unless you die of a heart attack.

Our scariest moment is when Michael makes a dental appointment for us to have our teeth cleaned in Naoussa. I think we're in trouble—the dentist doesn't speak much English and says that he is located near the place that serves *souvlaki*, which narrows it down to about 5,000 possible locations. I'm going to check my dictionary to see whether the English word "cleaning" translates into anything that sounds like "extraction" in Greek. When Michael hangs up the phone, we look at each other and, at the exact same moment, say, "You first!"

We finally get up the nerve and go to the dentist for a routine cleaning. It is a new concept in Greece to visit the dentist for anything less than a severe toothache (like the two other patients in the waiting room, suffering in great pain). Preventive dentistry? Unheard of! But he happily obliges us, pulls out an old-fashioned, sharp-edged metal scraper, and removes the plaque buildup from our teeth to the best of his ability. He is almost apologetic when he charges us US$15 dollars each for the service. He's probably thinking, "Those crazy Americans!"

And while our pesky new houseguest, the mouse, isn't scary, his existence is troubling. So far the score is Mouse 1—Michael 0. We locate the nest of the little mouse, which has been rattling in our pots and pans and paying occasional visits to us in the living room. It is inside the back of the washing machine (the machine was squeaking and it wasn't on). There is no way to get to it. Michael has pitted his well-developed, multi-degreed brain against the mouse's pea-sized brain, and he's a bit miffed that I keep cheering for the mouse.

There is a gruesome end to the mouse saga. We actually catch it in a glue trap, and Michael has to drown the poor little beast in a bucket of water to end its misery (as our friend in Greece whose name shall not be mentioned instructed us to do).

* * *

Capers, apricots, and peaches are now ripe for picking and plentiful at the markets. The tomatoes are even sweeter than they were when we first arrived, and a new growth of lemons has appeared on the trees. Artichokes are sometimes available, and we eagerly anticipate the ripening of figs and almonds.

The tourists disembark in droves off the ferries. They are mainly Germans and Swiss this month. We hear that the Italians are due next month. It's fun to sit by the port, sip a café frappe, and watch the hustle and bustle. The town undergoes a transformation in preparation for the tourist invasion: restaurants set their chairs and tables outside, particularly along the seaport. Traffic patterns change to accommodate the crowds. Certain streets have been converted to one-way or pedestrian-only walkways, which is a brilliant idea, considering that seemingly idle wandering is a Greek pastime.

A focus of local entertainment is the beach because foreigners love to fry in the sun. The whiter their skin, the more they love it. Topless is fashionable (among the foreigners, never the Greeks), and after-sun skin-care products that contain aloe are in great demand. But it's easy for us to escape the tourists, since our mountain abode is not exactly a happening place. The only reminder that they are here is that around five or six o'clock, we lose our water supply. The demand is so high that the water pressure drops and cannot reach us on the mountain. It returns around eleven at night. The main problem is flushing the toilets. The responsibility has fallen on Michael (sometimes it's good to be obsessive) to maintain a reserve of water, and I've worked out a system for washing the dinner dishes, so we have adjusted well enough. It is a bit like camping. In spite of this, we enjoy dinner on our terrace, where we gaze at sunsets that rival any in the world. We start off with a glass of *ouzo* and lots of ice (which turns the *ouzo* milky), fresh fish hot off our grill, add some grilled onions, peppers, and zucchini accompanied by bread and salad, and it equals (and sometimes excels) the local restaurants for fine fare.

The surf has finally warmed up, making swimming refreshing and addictive. There are several wonderful beaches; they become less crowded as you drive away from town. The clear and unpolluted water has some grasslike strips of seaweed—not at all unpleasant for swimming. Sea urchins line the rocks, but we haven't sighted any jellyfish. The restaurants have a good supply of octopus hanging from a clothesline in front of their outdoor tables along the seaport. Calamari are fresh and plentiful. Grilled fish is available, but more pricey, since the seas are somewhat depleted by the commercial fishermen. It's priced by the kilo, and the tradition is to go to the kitchen, pick out your fish, have it weighed, and then sit back down to anticipate its reappearance on your plate, grilled to perfection. We discover "tomato croquettes," which taste like conch fritters without the conch—just a marvelous taste of tomatoes, breading, and fresh herbs fried up in a little olive oil, served hot and bursting with flavor. Another of our favorites is octopus served cold as a salad, marinated in a lemon and oregano dressing with lots of fresh, crusty bread to dunk in the dressing. Pair this dish with a crisp, white local table wine, and you have an absolutely perfect lunch on a warm, sunny day, sitting under a bamboo awning in a cozy restaurant by the sea.

With the constant surprises of this new life, we learn to go with the flow. Here I am thinking I've got to jump into a hot shower while we still have water and slather tons of conditioner on my hair, which has become just like the wheat—dried out, sun-bleached, and due for a "threshing"—but then, and just like that, we lose electric power. Who cares? On Paros, life is grand!

CHAPTER 5

Greece to Turkey

A shroud has no pockets.

—Old Turkish Proverb

The only plan Michael and I made prior to coming to Greece was to sail around the southern coast of Turkey with our friends from Connecticut, Warren and Dana Cohn. A friend of ours had taken the trip twice and told us about the charter that Luce and Philippe Boisvieux run out of Marmaris, Turkey. It sounded so exotic and enticing; we booked it for seven days.

We depart at the end of May and need to exchange some money for Turkish lira, so we ask our Greek acquaintances on Paros how we might do it. Generally, the Greeks do not exchange their drachmas or US dollars for Turkish lira.

"The Turks killed my family," we are told by one agent, after which Michael and I realize we must be more careful with whom we discuss our travel plans.

There are no flights or ferry boats going directly to Turkey. We have to get to the European side of Cyprus first.

We receive travelers' advisories from the US State Department against going to Turkey because there are some riots and demonstrations occurring in parts of the country. Abdulla Öcalan, a founding member of the separatist Kurdistan Workers' Party (PKK), was arrested by Turkish security forces and sentenced to death. The sentence was ultimately commuted to life in prison when Turkey abolished the death penalty in its bid for European Union membership. The hapless Kurds have a worse reputation than the poor Albanians. Nevertheless, armed with a few American dollars and a woeful lack of knowledge about Turkey, we are excited and ready for what life may bring.

The timing of our departure from Greece is perfect. The American Consulate in Athens informs us that Greece is now instituting the European Union rules for temporary residency visas. We need to leave Greece and spend time in a non-EU country before our visas expire, or else we won't qualify for another three-month visa. Like most countries, the Greek government doesn't want people staying too long in a quasi-permanent resident situation by renewing a three-month visa time and again. Therefore, on the day our visa is due to expire, we plan to land on Turkish soil, in a place called Marmaris.

We have no idea what to expect. As the ferry nears land, I am awed by the view, and I look at Michael and say, "Let's keep an open mind about coming back here to stay for a while."

We have seen some pretty spectacular sights in Greece (such as Santorini, which we explored briefly), but this is something else. We see layers of enormous mountains that are heavily forested, green and lush. They descend steeply and end in a natural fresco of rust, brown, and gray rock along the water's edge, finally plunging into the crystal clear turquoise and cobalt blue waters of the Mediterranean Sea.

The serene coastline reveals no signs of civilization until we round a bend and pull into bustling Marmaris. The surrounding mountains protect the harbor, creating a safe, gorgeous inlet. These calm waters are home to some magnificent yachts, including our charter. We walk off the ferry and up to the customs window, pay for our entry visas— US$45 each—and have our passports stamped. We select a hotel (called Sariana) that is within walking distance of the marina and head that way. We find an ATM and insert our credit card, and I have a minor panic attack when the machine keeps spitting out money. I am convinced that Michael hit some wrong buttons and all our hard-earned savings are now coming out in Turkish lira. It turns out well, however. The exchange rate is 400,000 lira to a dollar; it's nice to be millionaires in Turkey! So far, so good. We have money, we have a hotel, and we've got four days before Warren and Dana arrive and our sailing trip begins.

We contact our sailing hosts, Philippe and Luce. After reassuring them that we are traveling light and have no intentions of sinking their boat, they invite us to dinner. We walk to the main strip in Marmaris, which is lively with small restaurants, discos, and shops of all kinds (in particular, Turkish rugs). We are introduced to some of the *traditional* Turkish fare, starting with *raki* (known as lion's milk), which tastes like *ouzo*, but perhaps not quite as sweet. Still, it delivers the same punch. The waiter serves a crisp local white wine and puts a plate of what looks like string beans on the table. We each take a bite of the beans, which turn out to be chili peppers. Rather quickly, our lips, tongues, and throats are aflame, and for several minutes we can only gulp wine. Philippe tells us, "They are good for the digestion."

The fresh veggies are terrific, with tomatoes even sweeter than in Greece. We eat a moist, tender white grouper—grilled whole, then split in half and deboned—garlic bread, and a dessert of fresh melon, cherries, and strawberries. During dinner, Philippe and Luce's longtime friend Taner joins us. He insists that Michael and I accompany him on a trip to his hometown of Muğla, about thirty minutes north of Marmaris, later in the week.

The next day, Michael and I rent a car and head up into the mountains to see some of the villages. The weather is perfect: sunny, clear, and comfortable. The road just out of Marmaris quickly heads up into the mountains, and we are negotiating hairpin turns through heavily forested mountains reminiscent of the Rockies. Our first stop is Turunç, which is at the base of the mountains. All the signs are in German and Turkish, and it proves to be a charming little village beside the sea. We choose a restaurant on the beach playing Elvis Presley songs, and somehow I end up dancing with the young, handsome waiter.

Phillippe had enlightened us: "The Turkish people will never say no. They will go to any length to get an answer for you."

Over the next two weeks, this becomes obvious. On our drive, we are already beginning to fall in love with the people and the country. We venture past some ancient stone farmhouses and a Turkish mosque, arriving in a little village called Bayir tucked in the mountains. As soon as we park our car, we are greeted by a young Turkish man who welcomes us with a big smile, walks us to his store, and brings us Turkish tea, called *çay*, served hot and sweet in small glasses. This is a delightful Turkish custom. You needn't buy anything (but of course we did—some Turkish spices and lemon toilet water, which is so refreshing on the skin). It is probably an insult to refuse the tea, so when in Turkey …

✳ ✳ ✳

Friday comes, and Taner, true to his word, picks us up at our hotel. Off we go to Muğla, a beautiful inland town known for its traditional architecture. We walk through an open-air market in the middle of town that's overflowing with goods like tomatoes, fruit, beans, couscous, cheeses of all kinds, and other mysterious items that I don't have names for. The Turkish vendors encourage us to have a taste of everything. Taner exudes happiness and contentment to show us the town where he grew up. An architect in his late forties, single and busy with his work, he is pleased to answer whatever questions we have. He is most curious about things in America—in particular, the "Monica Lewinsky thing" and how ridiculous he thought that was. The Turks *love* Bill Clinton, especially after his visit to Turkey. He also has questions about our court system, sports figures, and so on. We learn so much from Taner about Turkish customs, including some politics and other assorted tidbits of information. He has such a love for his country that it is a pleasure to listen to him.

We spend the rest of the day wandering through town. We tour the ancient Greek section, visit an historic Turkish house, and saunter past blacksmith shops and Turkish coffee houses, where women are not welcome. We ask Taner about the Turkish baths (*hamam*), at which point his face lights up and he says, "Let's go to the one here in Muğla. It is very traditional, and not touristy."

We enter the 600-year-old Turkish bathhouse, and a small Turkish man shows us to the dressing rooms upstairs and gives us each a cloth sarong, called a *pesternal*, to wrap around ourselves and a pair of rubber shoes. We follow Taner down the stairs and into the bath area. The room is constructed with marble from floor to ceiling and seems to have remained unchanged over the centuries. Steam rises from the baths.

An attendant points to a heated marble slab—called a *göbek tasi*—in the center of the room, on which two men are reclining. It soon becomes the "Gerber tushi" slab. There are three smaller rooms off the main room where several fountains run with warm water, and there are marble benches all around. The facility is naturally ventilated through openings in the dome on top. I imagine the thousands of conversations that could have taken place in here over the centuries. I am feeling a little uncomfortable, since I see no other women. I keep my bathing suit bottom on under the cloth *pesternal* and promise myself that I'm not getting naked for this deal. There are two attendants, wrapped only in the *pesternal*, who work on the other men. Michael, Taner, and I sit around *shvitzing* like crazy, and I finally begin to mellow out.

Taner looks perfectly at home, like a Turkish sultan. He takes *hamam* once every two weeks, which has been the custom of Turks since medieval times. Finally, one of the attendants points at me (yikes, I guess I'm first), and I lie on a marble bench, stomach down. He starts in with his loofah mitt, which is comparable to medium-grade sandpaper, and firmly sands the back of my body. He then slaps the marble with his towel, which I discover means "turn over." My wet *pesternal* must be in his way because he casually tosses it aside, but he seems pretty unaffected by the view. In any case, they speak no English, so having a discussion on this topic is pretty much out of the question. The brisk sanding continues, and I watch as my skin lands in piles on the floor around me. I am then thoroughly rinsed by my attendant with buckets of warm water poured on me, and the next phase begins—a large white cloth bag is filled with soapy water and the bubbles are squeezed through the fabric. He gently uses it to massage me. This is heavenly, and now I don't want him to stop! But alas, he points to a room where I am to shower off. With nary a good-bye, he briskly moves on to the next person. It isn't the typical spa treatment. It's more like a car wash.

Now that the three of us are cleaner than ever before, we are directed to yet another room. There, we are wrapped in dry, heated *pesternals* and have towels wrapped into turbans on our heads. We follow Taner upstairs to the "sitting room" and enjoy some cold drinks. A new camaraderie has formed between the three of us, as you might imagine. Several days later, Michael reads about the Turkish bath in a traveler's guide, which enlightens us.

> There are separate baths for men and women, or when there is only one bath house in the town, different days or times of the day are allocated to men and women.

I wonder if they still talk about the day that I desegregated the Turkish Bath House of Muğla!

We end this wondrous day at a restaurant in the countryside, owned by Taner's cousin. The chef prepares for us the fresh-caught shrimp that we bought earlier at the marketplace. We also dine on fresh swordfish, salads, appetizers, and of course, *raki*. We watch a huge stork land in its nest, high up in the rocks on the nearby mountain. Finally, Taner drops us off at our hotel—how he manages to drive on those curvy roads in the pitch-black darkness after copious amounts of *raki*—without killing us all—is remarkable!

Taner

Luce and Phillipe

Dana, Michael, and Warren

CHAPTER 6

Southern Coast of Turkey Sailing Excursion

A journey is a person in itself; no two are alike. And all plans, safeguards, policing, and coercion are fruitless. We find after years of struggle that we do not take a trip; a trip takes us.

—John Steinbeck

The Cast

Warren: Connecticut doctor known for the longest-distance house call ever recorded. Organizes his money in his wallet, most attentive to the Hellenistic era, incurable romantic, wins the award for IN-YOUR-FACE MOONING.

Dana: Magnificent sketch artist who is never sick, hikes like a mountain goat, wins the award for BIGGEST FAILURE AS SOUS CHEF, and ties for first place with Jean for MOON STUPID award.

Michael: Always brings up the rear, sarcastic quip artist, loudest night bird, and poet extraordinaire. Wins the award for KLUTZIEST DISEMBARKATION OFF A DOCK.

Jean: Spends inordinate amount of time in the Lost and Not Found and leaves Eveready bunny in her dust. Complexion is a combination of sulfuric mud and SPF#50 sunscreen.

Philippe: Captain, teacher, archaeologist, anthropologist. Always trying to outsmart the fish "more clever than me." Obsessive boat neatnik who designs ships and speaks five languages.

Luce: The Captain's wife. French charmer, gourmet chef, anchor person, plumber, and bathroom bailer. Keeps captain in line. Princess Pitawama reincarnate.

Kiki: Part dog, part Sherpa, part fish, part Turkish rug with burrs.

The Setting

Beginning of June, the Mediterranean Sea, southern coast of Turkey on the *Pitawama*.

Day One

It is Sunday morning, and at long last our sailing adventure is getting underway. Our dear friends Dana and Warren Cohn have arrived from Rhodes, Greece, on the hydrofoil. Philippe and his wife, Luce, originally from France, have been living in Turkey for the past twenty years. We meet them and Kiki, their wonder dog, at the harbor and are given a tour of our quarters on the boat where we will be living for the next seven days. The sailing vessel is a sixty-nine-year-old, fifty-foot wooden ketch named the *Pitawama*, which Philippe reconstructed. Philippe runs a tight ship, fitted so perfectly that there is not one clang or rattle when the boat is moored, even in the breeze. The teak deck is beautiful and reflects many hours of sanding and polishing. The boat handles "like a Ferrari," to use Philippe's words. It is an elegantly appointed craft.

We learn the dos and don'ts, such as toilet flushing—not one of us gets this right, and we need further instruction after we nearly flood the boat.

"No shoes are permitted," says Philippe, gesturing to the teak deck. He instructs us where to unpack and store our clothes.

I unpack Michael's stuff, and for the entire trip he cannot find a thing. Michael and I move into the forward cabin, which opens up to a double bed, with a hatch to the deck overhead—saving me from creeping claustrophobia. Warren and Dana sleep in the center of the boat in the living room, which converts into two twin beds. Philippe and Luce sleep up top on the deck under a tent. As soon as we settle in, our sailing adventure commences. We leave Marmaris harbor and head north, toward one of Philippe's favorite lunchtime anchorages. About three hours later, we anchor in a magnificent cove and jump in for our first swim in the Mediterranean. We lie on the smooth, sun-warmed dark lava-pebble beach for a short while. Back on board, we are served cold champagne, whole shrimp in the shells, rice, beans, eggplant dip, and a light dessert of yogurt blended with fresh raspberries. And this is for *lunch!* After this, we take a siesta on the boat, feeling like we have really pulled off something special. Midafternoon, we set out to sea, heading south, and sail to our evening anchorage, Amos Bay.

Watching Philippe and Luce work as a team is a real treat. They communicate in their native French but need very few words to get the job done. For each event, Philippe has the timing down perfectly, and Luce doesn't miss a beat. We offer our assistance on more than one occasion but are politely told to relax and let them do their thing. No argument here! We are being treated with the utmost respect and care. Once we arrive at Amos Bay, we don our hiking boots for a jaunt on land. Philippe wears old boat loafers, which are a step up for him. Apparently, he used to hike barefoot. We take the dinghy ashore and head up a rocky path for our first glimpse of ancient ruins. Kiki comes with us, as she does on all the hikes and swims, and Luce remains on board to prepare dinner. After about twenty minutes, we come across some Hellenistic walls, tombs, and a theatre perched atop an acropolis. Philippe takes great care to avoid the heat of the day; we visit the site just before sunset in order to capture the best light. We soon discover that Philippe is a professor of archeology and has studied these sites for twenty years, making many of the discoveries himself. We pinch ourselves in disbelief that we could be so fortunate to have Philippe as a guide. His French accent somehow adds to the whole educational atmosphere—we whisper among ourselves if we don't quite catch the meaning of a word because the accent doesn't land on its correct syllable, so as not to interrupt the great master with the small things. He walks at a rapid pace, which *most* of us are able to keep up with (refer to cast of characters), and we don't want to miss a word that he is saying. The ruins are just *there*, for all to enjoy. No fences, no signs, no special entries of any sort. This in itself feels unique to us, and really helps us to visualize the history as Philippe describes the time periods of the sites and the possible events that occurred.

We head back down and stop at an outdoor bar at Amos Bay to have a drink and pull the burrs out of our socks and other places. We are the only ones there. Poor Kiki is burr-covered from head to tail, but she doesn't seem to mind too much. Philippe says we have to get back to the boat, change into some nice clothes, and get ready to have Chinese food.

We are like, "Yeah, right. In the middle of nowhere, a Chinese restaurant."

We will eventually learn that there is no way that you can tell whether Philippe is kidding. He never elaborates on what the plan of the day is—he just gives us basic instructions, leaving us to guess what adventure he has in store for us.

This leads to our discovery of "sea soap." It is amazing stuff that smells like pine soap, is highly concentrated, and works with the seawater to thoroughly cleanse the body. Warren, Michael, and Dana lather up—in fact, over the next three days, wherever Dana swims, she is followed by a soap slick. After much rinsing and hysterical laughing, they are clean. I opt for the shower in the head, or shall I say, the head becomes the shower. Once I figure out that the spigot in the sink pulls out and becomes the showerhead, I hold it over myself and try to wash in an area that is two feet square. The spigot twists like an angry snake, and the toilet paper, towels, and everything else in the tiny bathroom gets soaked. I think next time I will join the others in the ocean for a bath with sea soap.

Clean and starving, we hop into the dinghy in our finest clothes (shorts and T-shirts, what else?), pull up to a dock about four minutes later, walk through an astonishing, well-tended garden at the water's edge that has torchlights set up around tables, and end up feasting on the best Chinese food any of us has ever eaten. We drink lots of *raki*, share stories, and begin to bond in a special way. We take the dinghy back, giggling like crazy, and settle in for our first night sleeping aboard.

Day Two

Around eight in the morning, we wake up from a pretty good night's sleep to the aroma of freshly brewed coffee. Breakfast on deck involves coffee, fresh-squeezed orange juice, yogurt, fresh fruit, honey and toast. Just perfect.

We spend the morning anchored in the cove, swimming and sunbathing, and have an exquisite lunch: potato salad, smoked salmon quiche, and fresh baked apricots with raisins and whipped cream. Taking a siesta on a boat with the gentle movement of sea, lulled by the soft wind, is pure ecstasy. Shortly thereafter, Philippe and Luce cast off for a windy, beautiful afternoon of sailing. I want to take over the helm, and Philippe lets me, sitting next to me just in case, and I handle this beautiful sailing vessel for an hour or so. I am exhilarated and wishing this day, this trip, this adventure might never end.

Early in the evening we come to Ali's Cape, another magnificent protected lagoon-type cove, and anchor for the evening. We set off on foot once again, not knowing quite what Philippe has planned for us. We hike up a narrow dirt path through thick pine forests for about thirty minutes without a soul in sight. Philippe makes sure that we keep up the pace so we can catch the sunset. We hear goat bells and eventually see several of the familiar critters scattered in the woods, all of them quite curious about us. We continue through the forest until we come to a clearing. The setting sun casts a warm, golden light on the mountaintop; we have come to Ali's mountain.

Ali and his family are nomads and longtime friends of Philippe. Ali's wife comes to greet us and hands me a newborn kid (a baby goat) that I hold cradled in my arms. Their young son, about five years old, carries another adorable baby goat but is too shy to come and visit with us. Philippe and Ali are so happy to see each other. They hug, and I can see their pure joy in having this moment together. It has been a year since Philippe last visited, and he wasn't certain whether Ali would still be in this part of the mountains. A few days later, we would have missed them. We are invited to join Ali in their seating area. We take off our shoes and step up onto an outdoor platform covered with tapestries and pillows, set under the canopy of a carob tree and filled with the intoxicating scent of wild oregano. We sit comfortably. Ali's wife pours lemon water on our hands for cleansing and then brings us *çay* served beautifully in glass cups. She serves us goat cheese, pine honey, olives, and soft flatbread made on a cooking sheet over an open fire. Water is served, which is probably the most precious of the offerings—water is carried in jugs by donkey from about seven miles away. The setting sun illuminates the hills across the clearing, and we watch as Ali's goats—a hearty, healthy tribe of them—prance freely and happily in the soft light. A donkey walks right up to where we sit and lets out a loud *hee-haw*, demanding to be served water immediately.

Philippe translates as we share stories. We are told that, in a few days, the families will combine their tribes of goats and move to a higher place in the mountains for better grazing.

"How can you identify your own animals?" asks Michael.

"These are my children," says Ali. "I watched each one of them being born."

When Ali discovers that Warren is a doctor, he asks about the headaches that he has suffered for all his adult life, sometimes twice a month. After a gentle and thorough discussion with him—Phillippe working as a medical translator—Warren is able to diagnose migraine headaches and suggests a medication that might offer some relief. Hearing the good news visibly moved Ali. Philippe is so appreciative of having been able to help his good friend that he develops a new respect for Warren. Warren politely asks if we can take some pictures. After promises are made that the pictures of the family will be sent to Philippe to give to Ali on his visit next year, we photograph Ali's serene, Madonna-like wife and try to capture in a photo the love and friendship between Ali and Philippe. The moon lights our pathway back to the dinghy as we quietly absorb what we experienced that evening. After our traditional sea bath, we sit down to a candlelight dinner: a salad of anchovies, smoked salmon, arugula, and tomatoes and a main course of rice, swordfish with hollandaise sauce, tomatoes with parsley, steamed mountain greens with lemon, and a couple of bottles of wine. For dessert, Luce baked us a scrumptious "fruit pizza" (apricots and cherries in a flaky crust). Hours later, we sit around under the full moon and talk about the life of the nomad Ali. Philippe is sad as he speaks of the imminent end to Ali's way of life. But, for now, we all agree that the day was magical.

Day Three

We have settled in nicely by now and actually manage to go one full day without screwing up the toilets. After breakfast, we enjoy a brisk morning swim, and off we go sailing to Siesta Beach. This cove has a neat cave for snorkeling. The water is clear but cold because of the fresh water from the high, chilly mountain that streams into the cove. The site is gorgeous, with pink oleander bushes lining the riverbeds that meander along the rocky cliffs. Philippe brings back an octopus for the larder—and cuts his finger in the process. But no problem. We had Doc-on-Holiday ready to fix up the Captain. Luce prepares another scrumptious lunch: fried calamari, red beetroot, string beans and cheese, wine, and fresh bread. In the evening, we head for the town of Göçek (pronounced "gercheck"). This is a very posh marina—yachts from all over the world, including what used to be Atatürk's pleasure craft. What a surprise to come around the coast and see lights and neon signs for restaurants and discos. Three days out, and we have already become unaccustomed to modern civilization. It is a good time to take advantage of it though. We are able to take hot showers at the marina and shop a little in Göçek, which has only one main street and can be toured in fifteen minutes flat.

Dinner takes place at Philippe's favorite restaurant, where they serve *traditional* Turkish food. Our table is outside, at the end of the marina and behind the main street. We order several appetizers: eggplant with chili sauce, yogurt with dill, and fried *aubergine*. The next course is a grilled white grouper, an extraordinary Mediterranean fish. In fact, as Philippe describes the fish to us, our waiter comes tromping up from the marina with a 200-pounder. Oh yeah, there is our dinner—real fresh! A little while later, Philippe has a stern conversation with our waiter in Turkish. It seems that the waiter opened a second bottle of wine that we did not order, and he had started to pour it into our glasses. Philippe tells him that this is not proper and is tantamount to taking advantage of tourists. Further, he informs him that he knows the owner of the restaurant and that such behavior is not in keeping with the fine service that is demanded by the owner. By the time Philippe is through with him, the waiter is thoroughly ashamed. I daresay he will think twice before opening a second bottle unless he has clearly been asked to do so. The tourist business is economically vital for Turkey, and they are constantly striving to overcome past bad press, such as from the movie *Midnight Express*. It is well after midnight, and we walk to the marina, get back on board, and snuggle down in our beds for a good night's sleep.

Day Four

Philippe and Luce do some food shopping at the local markets while we enjoy the morning in town. We return to the ketch for a late breakfast on deck in the harbor and then motor out to Sea Urchin Cove, also known as Aphrodite's Spa. After anchoring, we hop in the dinghy and end up in paradise. The spa features a natural hot tub amid huge boulders—water gently flows into a pool that had been formed in the hot lava rock, just right for soaking. There are sea anemones nestled on the rocks by the warm, clear water, and we harvest little snails to eat later.

The shoreline in this area consists mainly of small, smooth lava rocks that are scorched hot from the sun, so we don water shoes to protect our feet and take a stroll. The formations of the cliffs are remarkable, and the limestone rocks with stalactites are unlike anywhere else in the world. The natural rock above us seems to be painted in gray, brown, and red tones, lending the illusion of an expansive art gallery. The water at the shoreline flows over limestone rocks, the layered colors reflecting the sun to create a crystalline watercolor.

Lunch today consists of cauliflower with ginger, *mugver* (potato) pancakes, zucchini, grilled chicken, Greek salad, wine, bread, and fresh fruit.

After another zonked-out siesta, we sail farther east along the Turkish coastline, in and out of coves and inlets. Philippe rounds one and continues inland, rounds another cove, passes Turtle Island, and finally ends up in a cove that there is no way in hell I (or most human beings) could find again. Naturally, this is Philippe's favorite hideaway, known as Pirates' Cove. I can picture the old days (like maybe a couple of months ago), sailing by just as happy as can be, when out of nowhere a boat appears and fierce-looking pirates prepare to throw their anchor on your deck and come aboard, ready to rape, pillage, and God forbid take your SPF#50 sunscreen! We love the spot. Philippe's name for this is "Stairway to Heaven," since he found a stairway built out of rocks going up the mountain. He has searched the area many times over the years to see if there is a tomb nearby, but he has found nothing at all.

We put on our hiking boots, hit the dinghy, and once again set out to visit ancient ruins on an isolated island. High up on a rocky mountaintop are tombs and Byzantine structures with writings etched in the walls and a stone-covered archway over a path for protection from the heat leading down the mountain. Philippe describes the life and times during that period, and he is brilliant as usual. In fact, a small group of tourists wandering on the island has no idea of what they are looking at and take advantage of Philippe's history lesson too.

We climb down, looking forward to another gastronomical delight. We are not disappointed—but first, a surprise happens during our evening swim. It is dark out, and as we swim, the water lights up with phosphorescent plankton. They look like millions of underwater lightening bugs. The stars are duplicating this in the sky. Once we get dry, dinner is served—penne pasta mixed with butter and a little cream, red pepper flakes, smoked salmon, parsley and capers, Greek salad, and for dessert a strawberry pie. We stay on deck late drinking *raki* (Philippe says it is a good *digestif*, and who's going to argue with that?), watching the stars and enjoying the most perfect spot in the world.

Day Five

We leave Pirates' Cove early the next morning, heading back northeast toward Marmaris. The wind is quite strong, the sea's choppy, and we have to motor to reach our destination, which Philippe refers to as Moussa's Cove. Shortly after arriving, we put on our snorkeling gear, and Philippe points to an underwater tomb. It has a green coat of moss covering it and looks like it has been underwater for a very long time. We wonder who is buried in this tomb—it has no markings on it.

Back on board, Luce is ready for our return. Today, she whipped up a pizza (mustard spread, thin slices of cheese, tomatoes, capers, olives, and oregano, spread with olive oil and baked), potatoes fried in olive oil with red pepper flakes and garlic, and string bean salad with a mustard and olive oil dressing. I am amazed at the number of fresh ingredients she stores in this tiny little kitchen. We rest up well to prepare for a long evening hike.

Early in the evening, we take the dinghy across the small bay to Mystique's Island and hike past ancient tombs and up into the pine forest for a magnificent view of the tiers of mountains surrounding the Mediterranean Sea. Just past the pine forest, Philippe illustrates his personal approach to periodontal disease—fresh-picked sage leaves placed directly on the gums. I try this, but immediately spit it out. It tastes like one of Mystique's goats just peed on it. The field is full of sage, oregano, and bay leaf bushes as big as trees. Warren and Michael decide to perch and wait for the sunset at the ruins on the mountaintop. Dana and I are game for continuing on our hike with Philippe. Truth be known, Warren is still recuperating from the *digestif* of the night before, and Michael is greatly relieved to hang with him (recuperating from a touch of old-age syndrome).

The three of us continue on through the meadow, passing an ancient cistern big enough to walk into. We enjoy listening to Philippe chanting a Byzantine prayer inside the echoing space. As we walk farther, we hear the sound of goat bells, and Philippe's expression lets us know a surprise is coming. He picks up his pace (Dana's and my little legs working as fast as they can without slipping on the rocks), and then we hear the sound of a wooden flute. We find Mystique. We follow the sound, and as we come up to Mystique's home, three stunning wild horses come out from behind a hill and gallop right past us. What a sight to behold. Dana and I keep looking at each other in complete wonder. Philippe introduces us to Mystique, his wife and teenage daughter, and a family friend and her daughter. Once again, they greet Philippe warmly (especially the daughter, who obviously has a major crush on him). They kiss Dana and me cordially on each cheek. I'm sure they don't get too many visitors dropping in on them in this remote part of the world.

Located toward the center of a large meadow, under an ancient olive tree, the homestead has a separate small stone building for the kitchen. Their seating area is set up off the ground and covered by tapestries and pillows. After spraying orange toilet water on our hands, we are served refreshing sage tea (dried sage leaves in boiling water with sugar). Philippe and Mystique catch up on each other's lives, and Dana and I watch as a huge man on a little donkey comes to visit. He looks like Sancho Panza from *Man of La Mancha*. He shows us his saddlebag contents—it's stuffed full of baby chicks that he is bringing to his home in the mountains. Then Philippe and Mystique whip out their cell phones (Mystique's new toy) to program in each other's phone numbers. What a great commercial for Sprint.

It is starting to get dark, and Philippe is anxious to have us get a move on. We meet up with Michael and Warren; they enjoyed reminiscing about the good ol' days and watching a beautiful sunset. Back at the boat, we have a "full moon" sea bath. Sipping an aperitif of ice-cold vodka and olives, we have a lesson from Philippe on astronomy—is there anything this guy *doesn't* know? Then, we feast on filet mignon with peppercorn sauce. We have a salad of string beans, carrots, rice, feta cheese, tomato, and scallion, and top it off with crème brulée for dessert. The moon is full, the weather so clear and gorgeous, that Dana and I decide to sleep up on deck. Phillippe warns us we might wake up "moon stupid" and might also be bothered by bees at sunrise. We'll take that risk. Dana and I spend a good part of the night watching the moon travel across the sky. We wake up to the sound of roosters and goat bells and watch as the goats playfully come down from the hills toward the beach. We decide that "moon stupid" must come from an inability to function efficiently as a result of a lack of sleep, but we agree it was well worth it.

Day Six

At Lawrence Cove, we have to leave fairly hastily, since the winds are picking up. We make it to Pine Cove—a thick pine forest beginning at the coast and climbing up, covering the mountain. We freshen up (a sea bath, of course—we are hooked) and are told to prepare for a long evening's adventure, which includes dinner out. This time Luce is able to join us. Soon a large wooden Turkish boat appears; we board and begin our mysterious excursion. The water is calm as we motor past the Dalyan Delta, a long, golden sandy nature conservation area that is a refuge for sea turtles and blue crabs. We continue through a maze of channels around islands of bamboo reeds that look a bit like the Everglades to the ancient harbor of Caunos.

Caunos was an important Carian city by 400 BC. On the border with Lycia, its culture reflects aspects of both empires. We tie down at a small harbor, walk through the ruins of many civilizations, and end up on top of a mountain in an amphitheater. Over 2,000 years old, the well-preserved theater seats about 5,000 people. Dana, Luce, and Kiki mug for a few photo ops, and we continue on. On the hill above, there are remnants of an acropolis and a fabulous view of the surrounding countryside.

On our walk down, Philippe looks at us sternly and asks, "Do your eyes work?"

So, of course, we look up, and high on the cliff face are magnificent ancient Lycian tombs carved into the rock, one of the most famous sights in Turkey. We end our walk at a natural hot sulfur spring tucked in the hills and cover ourselves with therapeutic mud. I give myself a good facial with the black mud. I feel a bit perturbed because it evidently didn't rinse off very well, and everyone who looks at me during the course of the evening bursts out laughing.

We board our Turkish boat and enter a dreamy, tranquil world along the inlet in Dalyan, where restaurants line the waterfront, stopping at a lovely place where Philippe has prearranged dinner for us. An elegant table waits for us right on the dock, and so, as has become our custom, we proceed to have another spectacular fresh fish dinner. The evening's specialty is grilled sea bass, split down the middle and deboned, which goes very well with cold *raki*. Around midnight, we get back on our Turkish boat, and the young man captaining uses only a flashlight, turning it on quickly now and then to navigate us through the channels, around the bamboo, and past the delta flawlessly. We pass the carved tombs in the cliffs, lit up at night and simply spectacular. The plankton in the water sparkles, competing with the reflections of the stars. Actually, most of our group doesn't see this because they are passed out on the bottom of the boat. Michael is snoring, and Phillippe whispers to us, "That is a night bird." We can't believe that it is our last night of the trip, but what a grand finale.

Day Seven

Tough getting up this morning. *Raki* revenge. But we get up anyway, so we'll have time for lunch and a swim before heading into Marmaris. Philippe brings us to yet another incredibly beautiful spot to anchor, and we have a major farewell lunch on board. This time it is fresh sea urchin that Philippe has just caught, opened, and cleaned for us. It is the "caviar of the sea," and we love it. Then we have the octopus caught the day before in a vinaigrette marinade, served cold. This is followed by grilled lamb chops served with arugula and roast potatoes and, to top it off, a chocolate torte. Michael reads a poem to Philippe and Luce that he wrote for them, composed of some favorite thoughts that we all put together, truly capturing the essence of the week. There is not a dry eye in the bunch when he gets through. After the week-long sailing trip, the four of us spend five days in Santorini, the perfect place to reflect on the amazing sailing trip and our good friends before parting ways and heading back to our Paros haven.

Turkish Delight

In Southern Turkey, there plays a drama:
The continuing saga of *Pitawama*.
Philippe and Luce are captain and crew,
Able-bodied, tried, and true.

Enter the Gerbers, enter the Cohns,
About to sail to the great unknown
On this elegant craft of brass and teak.
We flirt with the sun as it dances behind peaks;
We swim in lagoons so crisp and cool
And bathe in the warmth of Aphrodite's pool.
We take siestas while gently rocking
As Philippe plans excursions, always shocking.

Down in the galley, Luce is at work
Creating the best of the French and the Turk.
Succulent swordfish, pastas, and pies—
Artistic presentations, a feast for the eyes.
Her skill with spices and flair with herbs
Wins the hearts and stomachs of the Cohns and the Gerbs.

O Captain, Our Captain, Philippe is his name,
A Renaissance man of widespread fame.
We walk in the mountains, stroll on the beach—
Antiquities everywhere, so much to teach.
Hellenist, Roman, Byzantine, Greek,
And even the families of Ali and Mistique.

Of course we should mention our four-legged mate,
The incredible Kiki, who does many things great.
She swims like a fish and hikes like a champ;
She walks up a ladder like it is a ramp.

For seven days we've sailed in bliss;
Important areas we did not miss
Thanks to Philippe, and thanks to Luce.
A more formidable voyage we could not choose.

But now our amazing trip must conclude
With heaping platters of fabulous food.

Dedicated to Philippe and Luce Boisvieux for their indispensable hospitality during our cruise May 30 to June 5, 1999.

Michael and Jean Gerber

Warren and Dana Cohn

CHAPTER 7

Next Stop: Switzerland

A good traveler has no fixed plans, and is not intent on arriving.

—Lao Tzu

Living in Paros has been a joy for us. The summer weather is perfect every day; we've settled nicely into the lifestyle and are comfortable. That's when Michael and I look at each other and say, "Time to leave."

There is just too much to see in the world, and we are ready for the next adventure. Besides, we know that we can't buy property in Greece, as the government makes it highly unattractive for foreigners to purchase land, homes, and automobiles.

Our original plan was to go to Istanbul. It fit into our ideal scenario of great weather, fascinating culture, geographic proximity, and inexpensive lifestyle. But then the political situation with the jailed Kurdish leader, Öcalan, heated up. Our decision was finalized when an article in the *International Herald Tribune* reported that Istanbul was being targeted by Kurdish fanatics, who sought to attract world attention to their cause by killing a few tourists. Instead, we decide to go to Spain and Portugal.

We need wheels but give up trying to buy a car in Greece. We locate an auto broker in Zurich from an ad in the *Herald* and are pleased to discover that we can buy a used car there, tax-free, and be on our merry way. We pack up our belongings—which still fit into two suitcases and day packs—and say good-bye to our friends on Paros, both people and animals. All this in three days—it's so nice to be mobile.

Our plan is to get the car in Zurich and head south to Barcelona to meet up with our son, Lee, and his girlfriend, Melissa, who will be traveling in Europe. After that, we plan on driving to Portugal. We start our journey east by ferrying from Paros to Athens, and then we fly to Budapest and on to Zurich. The afternoon we arrive in Zurich, we go directly to the office of the car broker, Peter Iczkovits, and for the next three days we complete the process of buying a 1991 Subaru 4WD minibus. Peter is a delightful character, an orthodox Jew from Israel with ten children.

The car has to pass inspection by the Swiss authorities before he can sell it to us. The Swiss inspection is drastically different—no surprise—from the Miami auto inspection. They put the car through a number of tests, using sophisticated equipment in a spotlessly clean facility. This is one reason why we decide to buy a car in Switzerland (versus Holland, where you can also buy tax-free).

The car flunks the inspection the first time around. We join Peter on a scavenger hunt for various parts, getting a taste of the beautiful Swiss countryside along the way. Peter drives like a complete maniac. We are at his mercy, staying in a pricey hotel (one of the less expensive ones in Zurich, the St. George, about US$120 a night), praying each day that the stupid car will pass inspection. During one of our excursions, Peter stops at his favorite kosher restaurant and buys us what turns out to be the best lunch that we have in Zurich. He seems to know everyone in town. He is as anxious as we are to put the car in order and get us out of his hair. Given the amount of time he spends on us, he is not making a whole lot of money on this transaction—the car only costs us about US$4,500, including insurance. All the paperwork is done from his office: insurance, registration, and license. Once it passes inspection, the actual process is easy. We grow fond of Peter and his eccentric personality.

While we wait for our transaction with Peter to conclude, we tour Zurich on foot. Our initial reaction is sticker shock, since we just came from Greece. For example, a McDonald's Happy Meal—a quarter-pounder, fries, and a coke—for two costs US$18! Not such a happy meal after all. We go to the movies one night because we are absolutely craving a good flick, and the seating is reserved, with your choice of three sections, the least expensive being US$11 per seat. The theater is spotlessly clean, the people are oh-so-civilized (how do they eat popcorn without spilling a kernel?), and the sound system is a most welcome change from the Greek outdoor cinema. We see an American movie, *The Matrix*, with German and French subtitles—welcome to Switzerland. At intermission, everyone exits the theater in an orderly fashion to have a smoke, reentering at a precise moment for the second half to begin.

* * *

The streetcars in Zurich are a marvel. You can easily get anywhere. The streets are sparkling clean, and there is no need for policemen. God forbid you do something wrong, like cross where there is no crosswalk. Shame on you! The nearest horrified Swiss person will instantly castigate you. But on the other side, Zurich is pedestrian friendly—if you step into the street at a crosswalk, the cars must stop or else be ticketed. Michael has so much fun testing this out—stepping with one foot onto the street, then pulling it back to the sidewalk, and then again onto the street. He just can't believe that the cars will consistently stop, but they do. It is so different from Greece, where a pedestrian is a moving target for the auto driver. The Swiss have many rules that everyone obeys without question—it sounds a bit uptight, but we came to appreciate a country where everything works like, um, a Swiss watch.

Finally, three days later, the car passes inspection. We pack up and head toward Portugal, via Barcelona. First, we make a stop and buy some basic camping gear. We have our minibus, and by God we are going to do some camping! We are in our "superannuated hippie" mode. As a friend of mine said, "Once you have achieved this level of consciousness and spirit, you cannot then downgrade to a lesser form."

Our first destination is the Pilatusblick Hotel, just outside of Lucerne, which Peter recommended to us. It sits high up on Pilatus Mountain in the Swiss Alps, overlooking Lake Lucerne. We soon learn that our cute little Subaru has as much power going uphill as a tired old Greek donkey with its wooden saddle loaded with bales of figs, a Greek farmer, and his typically heavy Greek wife. We are forced to sit back, enjoy the scenery, and take our time getting to Barcelona through the Alps.

The hotel is fantastic. Cows graze on the green hillside. Swiss wooden chalets dot the hillsides, and the village on the shore of Lake Lucerne features large, pristine wooden gingerbread-style homes, landscaped with perfectly tended geraniums, sunflowers, and other colorful varieties. Church bells ring, the cowbells chime throughout the hills, and the air is fresh and cool. It is a lush, green sensory overload after the dry earth tones of Greece in the summer.

After a brisk walk up the hill the next morning, we toss in our suitcases, hop in the bus, and turn the key … nothing. Dead. Not a peep from the engine. The hostess of the hotel calls her favorite mechanic, who arrives within five minutes. He removes a couple of parts from the engine and manages to start it up, and we drive down the hill to his shop. For the rest of the day, we have two Swiss mechanics performing surgery on the engine. Parts come out and go back in. Heads are scratched and chins are rubbed as they think it through. At last, the operation is complete, and they say that we are good to go. We drive for about five minutes, turn around, and go back to the shop, where more surgery is required. They finally admit that it is as good as it is going to get, and they say, "Good luck!"

We've lost the better part of the day, so we drive for two hours to a beautiful resort village on the Brienzersee called Bönigen. We check into the Baren Gasthaus and have dinner nearby—bratwurst, beer, and *kartoffeln*, a true initiation into German Swiss cuisine. We have a good night's sleep, tucked in under our cozy *dekas*—warm down comforters. The next morning, ready to continue on our journey to Spain, we once again throw in the suitcases, turn the key, and … nothing. Our hostess calls her favorite mechanic and—no lie—before Michael is off the phone and out the door, the mechanic is there. Having car trouble and two times in a row having a mechanic show up within about thirty seconds? As distraught as we are, we marvel at the speedy service.

The car has to be towed this time, with a rope that breaks and has to be retied three times, but we eventually make it to the mechanic's shop. By then it is lunchtime, and everything is closed for a couple of hours. Later that afternoon, Christian, the mechanic, says he can't fix it, but that he has a friend named Bruno in nearby Interlaken who is an electronics expert. He recommends that we contact him. He does manage to get the car started and insists that he lead us there in his vehicle, in case we get into trouble. He won't charge us anything because he says he can't fix it. We force him to take a few francs, since he spent the entire day on our behalf. We arrive at Bruno's in Interlaken, and since it is five o'clock on a Friday, he can't do anything until Monday.

Barcelona is beginning to seem more like Mission Impossible to Mars. We are a bit concerned because the hotels are so expensive. We have no idea how long it will take to fix our cute little pain-in-the-ass car. We leave the car in Bruno's shop and walk into town to find a hotel, finding an "inexpensive" one for US$100 a night—no view, just a bed. Breakfast is included, if you like bread and wurst. About then, I try hard to remember why I left Greece. All that bullshit about wanting new adventures and embracing our wanderlust—what were we thinking?!

Over a couple of Rugenbräu beers (the popular local brand), we contemplate our situation. We aren't setting any records getting to Spain; that is for sure. We are stuck in the middle of Switzerland at the foot of the ice-capped mountain, the Jungfrau, a short hop away from the charming village of Grindelwald and a few minutes' walk to the crystal blue lake called Thunersee, in what has to be one the most extraordinarily picturesque places in the entire world. We rethink our situation. So what if we are at the mercy of our Subaru and Swiss mechanics? We decide to deploy some of the camping equipment we purchased and soak in the beauty that is surrounding us.

Our vagabond hearts restored, we eventually find a campground called Sackgut in a woodsy area along a river that has tents for rent, fully equipped with a stove, cots, pots and pans, dishes, and electricity for a mere US$52 a night, with fresh bread available in the morning for a couple of extra bucks. This is camping that we could deal with for a few days. We set up our new home, enjoy strolling around Interlaken, and bask in the view of the mountains right behind the campsite.

Monday comes quickly. We return to Bruno's to check on the car. Both the car and Bruno are gone, so we walk to the other end of town to the Subaru dealer to see about the possibility of trading in the ailing car we owned for less than a week. Lo and behold—there is our Subaru! Bruno couldn't fix it, so he had towed it over to the dealer's garage. The owner, Holk Oertel, has snow-white hair with a moustache to match and a friendly demeanor. We are immediately comfortable with him. He assures us that the car can be fixed, but he asks if we could leave it there for a few days. We figure his garage has been around for twenty-five years and specializes in Subarus, so we tell him to keep it until it works.

* * *

Michael and I have received another lesson in flexibility. We revise our plans and decide to take the train to Barcelona to meet up with Lee and Melissa and then come back to Interlaken, pick up the car, and head to Portugal from there. We enjoy two more nights in the campground, walk to the train station, and off we go to sunny Barcelona for three nights and four days. By this time we have befriended the resident campground owner, and she volunteers to let us keep our bags in her home while we visit Spain. She is so concerned about us making the early train that she wakes us up at six o'clock in the morning to make sure we are up. Oops, it is the wrong day—but it is awfully nice of her anyway! We are finding the Swiss people to be absolutely wonderful, and we enjoy our "captivity."

The train departs Interlaken at 7:05 a.m. and arrives in Barcelona at 7:25 p.m. We have a great overview of the Swiss and French countryside, and the trip goes smoothly. We meet up with Lee and Melissa at the Oriente Hotel on the main tourist avenue, called La Rambla. The first day, we watch several street mimes dressed up in creative costumes and makeup—soldiers, dancers, chess players—who manage to freeze in their positions for an eternity, until someone drops a coin in their hat, at which point they allow themselves a shift in position. Unfortunately, there is a seedy side to this location of the city. Three gypsy women single out Michael and try to get into his waist pouch to steal his wallet. He senses what they are up to, but even so, it isn't easy to peel them off his body. Finally, he has to shove them away, while Lee yells at them in Spanish.

The architecture of Barcelona is fascinating. The highlights, other than visiting with our kids, include the Joan Miró museum, the Picasso museum, and the magical garden designed by Antonio Gaudí. Lee's high school friend Ian, who happens to be traveling in Europe, communicates with us via e-mail, and we are able to visit with him as well. We all walk to the pier and have a paella dinner at the Port Vell.

Four days later, we head back to Interlaken. The train is about an hour late, overflowing with people who are crammed into the seats and clogging the aisles. The crowd is mostly comprised of young backpackers who are remarkably calm and accept the situation. We manage to squeeze into seats with four Aussies—best mates who keep us entertained with their stories.

We just barely make our connection in France for the long haul to Geneva, a night train running from midnight to 8:30 a.m. We have reserved seats for this, so we figure we are in business. They call them "sleeping compartments," but there is no way I can sleep on these seats. There are six seats per compartment—three on each side, facing each other. Three polite Russian guys who speak no English join us in the compartment. As we sit face-to-face, our knees touch, though in some cases, we have to intertwine our legs with our travel mates to fit. One side has windows; the other has sliding doors leading to the walkway through the train car. The five of us cozy up for the night and try to sleep. The Russians take turns leaving the compartment to smoke in the hallway. It is a long, long night. The next day, we miss our connection but make up for it by taking the Golden Panorama Express, starting at Montreux and traveling through some of the most gorgeous countryside and villages imaginable, such as Gstaad and Zweisimmon.

* * *

Our train finally arrives in Interlaken at around three o'clock Monday afternoon, and we head straight for the Subaru shop. Holk tells us that the car is fixed and working well. In our absence, he has been in touch with our car broker, Peter Iczkovits, and Peter says that he will pay the US$900 to repair the car because it was, in fact, his mechanic who screwed up the carburetor, and he feels responsible. This is unbelievable. Holk will not take any money from us.

"How do you know Peter will pay you?" asks Michael.

Holk replies, "Because he is Swiss!"

In further conversation with Holk's wife, Margrith (pronounced "Margreet"), we discover that the top floor of their Swiss chalet is for rent. It's a one-bedroom apartment located just on the outskirts of town, in Unterseen, within walking distance of just about everything. It's also at the base of a mountain, with hiking trails starting right next to the house. The charming hundred-year-old wooden chalet, nestled in gardens with an array of flowers, vegetables, and apple trees, has furnished rooms and a modern kitchen. The outdoor balcony has a little bistro table, a couple of chairs, and a view of the Jungfrau. The Jungfrau (translating to "maiden/virgin"), stands at 4,158 meters (13,642 feet), one of the main summits of the Bernese Alps, located between the northern canton of Bern and the southern canton of Valais, halfway between Interlaken and Fiesch. Together with the Eiger and Mönch, the Jungfrau forms a massive wall overlooking the Bernese Oberland

and the Swiss Plateau, one of the most distinctive sights of the Swiss Alps. The Oertels occupy the first floor, and Herr and Frau Stalder have been renting the second floor from them for many years. Upon seeing the top floor apartment, we fall in love with it immediately. They give us a very reasonable rate, and we commit to rent it. It will be available for us August 20. With that, we have literally managed to make lemonade out of a lemon!

* * *

We have three weeks before we can move into the Oertels' chalet, and we decide to take full advantage of the warm weather and drive through Switzerland to France, spending most of the time in Provence—camping! Hey, we're tough; we're cool. We're superannuated hippies, right? But can we bend over far enough to get in and out of a tent without rupturing something vital? We are willing to try.

We load up the Subaru with our new camping gear, including a tent that the salesman demonstrated could be set up in about thirty seconds. We bought the all-important high-tech, self-inflating, guaranteed-to-prevent-arthritis pads for under the sleeping bags; a butane stove; some camping pots and pans; a super-warm, lightweight comforter; and pillows. We feel ready for anything.

The roadways in Switzerland and throughout France are excellent. Signs are color-coded and well-placed, and the roads have clean rest areas with picnic spots along the way. We drive into a dreamworld: cows grazing on the light green pastures, evergreen trees and lakes around every bend, and splendid Swiss houses dotted with colorful flowers all set against a background of the magnificent Alps. Our Subaru is hangin' in there, and our first stop is just outside of Fribourg in the French part of Switzerland, at a four-star campsite called La Foret. Private, clean, with hot showers, washing machines, a pool, tennis courts, a restaurant, and even an ironing board. This is the campsite of our dreams, all for US$12 a night. You've got to love the Swiss.

The campgrounds are situated at the edge of a thick forest with a narrow walking path winding through it, sculptures carved from the tree trunks lining the paths. This is beyond what we'd hoped for—or even imagined. We set up camp, open a bottle of wine, cook dinner, and enjoy the outdoors in this surreal environment. It just proves that sometimes the simple things are the best. Later, Michael snores so loud that the tent vibrates but fortunately doesn't collapse.

The next day we drive a short distance to Gruyere, spend a couple of hours going through the castle, and have a picnic lunch on the hillside. We continue south to Aigle, passing the most perfectly groomed vineyards we've ever seen. In Greece, the vines lie on the ground, since the earth is dry and the sun is hot. In Switzerland, they are cultivated on precisely even stakes in rows along steep terraces, creating artistic vistas. The farther south we get, the cheaper the wines become until it makes no sense to drink water at all. Our third day out, we cross the border into France and are now in the French Alps. We drive through Annecy to a little village called Alby-sur-Chéran and find a campsite on a farm, with only a few campers and cows in residence among the apple trees. We love it.

Back in the village, we walk the couple of streets that comprise the town center and find a *boucherie*. The only French word I know is *oui*, but my habit of expressing myself by using my hands, rolling my eyes, and smiling like crazy is perfect for fooling just about anyone into thinking that I understand everything they say. Of course, I have no idea of what I might have purchased. (Was that lamb, veal, or hog snout in this *paté?*) But the country people are tolerant, warm, and friendly. We go into the ever-present *patisserie* and stock up on baguettes. Then we discover that, as in Switzerland, every campsite throughout France has fresh bread that you can order the night before.

The first night on the farm, a deluge of rain sends apples dropping out of the trees and pounding on our little tent. It's comforting to know the tent can hold up under the most extreme snoring and apple-dropping conditions. They've improved the materials of tents from the old Army canvas ones. We stay dry and cozy, listening to the soothing patter of raindrops.

We spend a couple of days in this area and make some wonderful discoveries. In Rumilly, we walk along the famous Gorges du Fier and visit the Château du Montrottier. The Gorges du Fier is a remarkable natural curiosity: a very narrow and deep gorge that you can visit via a bridge attached to the side of a rock. According to local legend, Count Montrottier was worried about the chastity of his wife, Diane. He ordered a young man, a little page, to monitor it. The boy, secretly in love with the beautiful damsel, complied and began to watch her every move. He then surprised the beautiful Diane while in the arms of Count Pontverre. The little page no longer felt love but hatred toward the girl. In revenge, he told Count Montrottier, who organized a plot to trap the couple. Count Pontverre fled for his life on a horse. The little page, determined to catch up, firmly clung to the tail of the steed. But Pontverre dragged him up above the Fier and cut off the tail of his horse. The young man fell and disappeared below, at the bottom of the gorge. Since that time, the inhabitants of the valley sometimes hear distant groans arising from the gorge. Some say it is the wailing little page, who mourns his lost love.

We find an Internet café that is located in a cave-like structure built in 1533. I love the stark contrast of the high-tech equipment and the medieval building. Perhaps it is not so strange for Europe though.

We say our farewells to Alby and continue south toward Aix-en-Provence, stopping at Monestier DeClermont to camp for a couple of nights. Next to our campsite is a hiking path that leads to a chapel on top of a hill. Quite pleased with ourselves as we hike for a mile up a steep hill, we are suddenly passed by a lady who has to be close to eighty years old, her arms full of groceries and walking a dog. A humbling experience! In the evening, we walk to a restaurant inside the Hotel Piot, built a few hundred years ago, and have a *trés magnifique* dinner of fresh trout, followed by a dessert of raspberry *tarte* and *crème caramel*. The patisseries in this area are exquisite, and in the mornings, you will see just about everyone in the village carrying at least one baguette in their arms, still warm from the oven.

We drive into Sisteron and end up staying for three days. At lunchtime during our first walk into town, we listen to Edith Piaf piped through one section where there is an abundance of outdoor cafés. We immediately fall in love with Sisteron.

The stores brim with table linens in the traditional pattern of Provence, and with gorgeous pottery of all shapes and sizes. Since I don't have a home to buy stuff for, I enjoy looking, but nothing comes with me. In truth, I discover a sense of freedom in not thinking about material things, gathering experiences instead.

We drive farther south to Aix-en-Provence, with its quaint, cobbled streets and alleyways full of upscale stores, bakeries, cafés, and churches. We walk for hours, "rent" a table at a sidewalk café, and enjoy the ambiance of this exquisite French city.

❊ ❊ ❊

We choose our next village because the name sounds so enchanting—L'Isle-sur-la-Sorgue. This turns out to be a small provincial city of about 18,000 inhabitants, located twenty minutes out of Avignon. We pride ourselves on perfect timing—the town, in the midst of its annual antique fair, has tables and booths set up throughout the town center. People from all over the world have come to this event, and we are swept up in the excitement of it all. Sunny, clear weather makes the day perfect. Surrounded by rivers and canals of clear green cool rushing water from the mountain springs, L'Isle-sur-la-Sorgue earned its name. Huge trees shade the parks, which are busy with pedestrians, baby strollers, artists, and singers. Artfully restored old buildings painted in ochre tones line the streets. The center of town has quaint little restaurants and cafés. There are narrow canals weaving in and around the town with bridges for pedestrian crossing, adding to the charm. It feels dreamlike. Sunday is flea market day, and in addition to the antique show, there are booths for selling crafts, clothes, fresh veggies, spices from Provence, cheeses of all sorts, fresh bread, and local wine. Fresh lavender bunches fill the air with the fragrance of earth and sun. If we were to choose a place in France to stay for a period of time, it would be L'Isle-sur-la-Sorgue. It has the right mix of sophistication, beauty, charm, and location.

We take a canoe trip on the Sorgue River, which gets off to a rather dramatic start since the instructions given to our canoe group are in French. We think, *no problem, we know how to paddle a canoe, for goodness' sake.* So we get in, figure we'll get in front of the crowd, and soon discover the river has a system of locks with a thirty-foot drop-off. Fortunately, the group leader catches up with us just in time to explain in broken English that you do not paddle over this in your canoe—you get out of your canoe and walk down some steps on the edge, and he will push the empty canoe over the top. You then retrieve it on the lower level in water about a foot deep, icy cold and slippery as hell, which is certainly a better plan than flying off the top of the lock.

We go on several excursions during this stay. The countryside of Provence has villages perched on the hillsides, with château dating from the as far back as the twelfth century. Many of them are constructed with dry stone walls, perfectly carved and balanced without the use of any mortar. One particularly wonderful discovery is Roussillon, which is known for its cliffs streaked with ochre colors, ranging from the brightest yellow to the deepest red. Painted in these natural colors, the buildings of this hilltop village and the churches with bell towers form a skyline that makes us feel as if we're entering Disney's Magic Kingdom. Ochre is mined in the nearby Ochre Trail, a fascinating forty-five-minute walk through earth pillars. For centuries, artists have used pastel crayons and paints made from this substance.

Nestled in the hills of Les Alpilles, we come to Saint-Rémy-de-Provence, a lovely village full of narrow medieval alleyways with fountains and shady squares and wonderful buildings. The town is forever associated with Vincent van Gogh, as this is where he checked into an asylum for a year (1889) in Saint Paul de Mausole Monastery. He completed 150 paintings during his stay, including *Live Grove* and *Starry Night*. We then visit the manor of the famous Marquis de Sade (now the Musée Archéologique). St. Remy is also the birthplace of Nostradamus.

On to Avignon—the great walled city. We simply drive by it, deciding we will need to come back and stay within its walls for several days to fully appreciate it.

We turn our gerbil-powered Subaru toward home, Interlaken, taking a more westerly route to complete the circle through Lyon in order to do our last food shopping in France before crossing the border. We will miss the food—the wonderful country *pâtés*, the Pim's cookies we've become addicted to, the wide selection of yogurts, beautifully displayed fresh vegetables and fruit, and of course the bread and wine.

* * *

Back in Switzerland, we camp near Montreux, spend a few hours touring the Château Chillon, walk along Lake Geneva, and soak up the view of the Alps in the distance. The weather has turned miserable; it is rainy and cool. We have dinner at a small, charming restaurant with a wood-burning fireplace and spend hours lingering over our food with lots of wine. We chum up with the owner before going back to our campsite. We have to remember we are back in Switzerland, not France—as Michael quickly finds out. You see, in France the bathrooms and showers are marked for men and women, but nobody pays any attention to these distinctions. Everyone just uses whatever is available.

So, on this rainy night, Michael follows me into the ladies' bathroom and shower area since it is closer than the men's room. He no sooner goes into the bathroom stall than a naked lady walks out of the shower, up to the sink, and begins brushing her teeth. To prevent her embarrassment, I try to keep Michael in the stall, waiting for an opportune moment when he can quickly escape unnoticed. He, however, sees no reason for concern, and he walks out slowly past the naked lady.

Another difference between French and Swiss facilities—apparently the French don't use toilet paper. There are no dispensers in the stalls, and no soap dispensers either. The French are a lot messier, in contrast to the Swiss (particularly the German Swiss), who are obsessive about cleaning up their sink and shower areas.

After an incredible three weeks of traveling through Switzerland and France, we settle into Holk and Margrith's Swiss chalet and unpack for the first time in a month. I now have a real kitchen with a real refrigerator and a real bed. Oh yes, this is good. I'm home again! I have a nest.

Swiss mechanics operating on our minibus

Jean, Lee, and Melissa with Michael in Barcelona

Aix-en-Provence

Life in Switzerland

You have brains in your head. You have feet in your
shoes. You can steer yourself in any direction you
choose. You're on your own, and you know what you
know. And you are the guy who'll decide where to go.

—Dr. Seuss

Paragliders sail through the skies around Interlaken. Michael and
I watch them in awe. It's mesmerizing to see them floating in the air,
their colorful, arc-shaped parachutes moving across the blue sky and the
green trees on the mountains. When Michael asks me what I would like
for my birthday, I am ready with my answer, and off we go to sign up for
a jump. On the appointed morning, we go to the designated meeting
spot, but the flight guide says it's too cloudy.

"We could get disoriented," he says, and I start imagining we will
crash into the mountains or be impaled on a pine tree or land in the
Brienzersee (a lake so cold, the fish are already frozen). He says, "How
about we wait for a clear day?"

No argument from me. The next five days are fogged in.

Finally we get a clear day and make the call. We meet up with
Robbie, who will be my tandem-jumping guide. Robbie is a native
of Switzerland, in his late thirties. He speaks English well and sports
some grungy-looking dreadlocks. I like him immediately. He's had
lots of paragliding experience and the proper Swiss certifications; I
am pumped. Tourist season is over, and I am the only one scheduled
that day. Michael will await my landing in the middle of the park in
Interlaken, camera ready for action.

"We're good to go," says Robbie enthusiastically.

Robbie and I drive to the top of the mountain in Beatenberg. We hike about five minutes to a clearing in a farmer's field. Standing before a spectacular view, we are facing the Alps (the Eiger and Jungfrau, the most recognizable), and the Thunersee is straight down below us. The cows on either side of the clearing have seen it all before; they barely glance up from their grazing. We approach a short rubber runway laid on a grassy meadow, which heads steeply downhill for maybe twenty or thirty feet, ending at a little fence. Beyond the fence, the land drops off dramatically. Robbie lays out the parasail, untangles all the strings, and attaches the sail to his harness with belay rings. We attach my harness to Robbie, for better or worse. The procedure is this: we take a few jogging steps downhill together, and when we feel resistance, we start running in order to fill the sail with thermal currents, which are created when the wind rushes against the sun-heated rocks of the mountains. Because hot air rises, we will be lifted up and flying. I don't want to sound like a fool or like I am having second thoughts, but I do ask, "What happens if we're not airborne by the time we reach the fence, which seems awfully close?"

Robbie says, "If we're not airborne by then, I must have screwed up, and we're in big trouble."

I giggle a little, pretending that I think that is pretty funny, as we wait for the cloth telltale on a post nearby to show us when the wind is coming straight up the mountain, the best direction for takeoff. Within minutes, it is go time.

I am so busy concentrating on putting one foot in front of the other and not falling flat on my face that I have no time to be scared. We start jogging—one, two, three, four—feel the wind resistance and jog a quick one, two, three, four, five—and *whoosh*, we are airborne! It is indescribably exhilarating. I position the seat under my butt, sit back, and am as comfy as can be. I look around and watch as the cows below become miniatures, just as we catch a thermal that lifts us up, up, and away. We sail past the blazing fall colors of the trees and then draw close to the mountain to try to catch more thermals to prolong our magical flight. As we round a mountain, I see the village of Interlaken far below in all its perfect glory—and then I take over the controls. Steering surprises me in its simplicity. I don't feel much pressure against the sail; I just pull down on one side while I raise my arm to lift the other. Robbie takes over the controls when some buildings come into view, and I spot Michael, a little dot in the middle of the field, our target for landing.

Robbie thinks he'll give me a few last-minute thrills, and we twirl like mad three or four times. Just as my stomach reminds me of what I ate for breakfast, we smooth out and head for Michael.

We secure a perfect landing. Michael gets the picture and we avoid the cows—and, more impressively, the cow patties. I help Robbie spread the sail in the field in order to fold it, and *whoops!* I stumble back into a humongous pile of cow shit—fresh, wet, slimy, and stinky. Nevertheless, my spirit soars from the twenty minutes or so of flying; I have such a wide grin on my face that there are bugs in my teeth. Nothing could muck up the experience I just had. It was an unforgettable birthday.

* * *

We return to the United States in October to attend Lee's wedding, which I'll succinctly describe as three weeks of frivolity with friends and family and the opportunity to meet Lee's new in-laws. Michael and I feel blessed by this moment in time when our children and Michael's parents are healthy in both mind and body, and we are all able to be in the same place at the same time. To top it off, we attend the wedding of the daughter of our dear friends and occasional travel mates, Warren and Dana Cohn. It is a uniquely loving celebration, and we are so glad to be part of it.

We take advantage of a few things in the States: the movie theater, the easy access to a variety of ethnic restaurants (particularly Thai and Japanese food), television in English, football, and the news channels. We quickly catch up with it all and feel like we could go another year or two without missing any of that. The *International Herald Tribune* has done a good job of keeping us up on the news while abroad, while being much more objective than the American news media. We shop for books, a few clothing items, drugs, and cosmetics, mainly because it is more comfortable for us to shop for them in the States and certainly less expensive than in Switzerland. After catching up on dentists, doctors, and business appointments, we are ready to continue on our journey.

Surprisingly, we don't feel like we are home in the States, just visiting. I think my new definition of "home" is wherever our stuff happens to be. I would never have dreamed that after being abroad for more than seven months I would be less than eager to go back to the States. I hadn't experienced the wonders of traveling and living abroad, and now I feel a sense of urgency. I realize it won't last forever—I want to soak in as much as I can and savor every minute.

Twenty-six hours of travel brings us back to Interlaken. When we step off the train, the weather is cool and the trees are changing to autumn colors. Our rented chalet is a five-minute walk from the station. As we arrive, we grab a couple of ripe apples off the tree in the front yard and exchange moos with the cows in the field next door, who come right up to the fence to welcome us home.

Our landlords, Margrith and Holk, invite us for dinner that evening. We bring the wine and salad fixings, and Margrith whips out four fresh trout that she ordered from the fishmonger that day. She prepares it simply by poaching the whole fish with some herbs and serving it with melted butter, salt, pepper, and ground nutmeg. We skin the fish and easily remove the bones. It is the best trout we've ever eaten. On the side are boiled, buttered Yukon gold potatoes and a fresh salad. Dessert is baked meringue filled with ice cream and topped off with a dollop of fresh cream that Holk whipped up. Clearly, Europeans don't give a damn about calories. They are in it for the taste, and there ain't nothin' like the real thing, baby. We discuss how Americans are obsessed with diets and weight watching—they visited Florida a few years ago and were astonished at how many Americans were grossly overweight. After dinner, we take the customary one-hour walk with them and their dog, Lisa. We are deeply grateful to be back.

Michael and I are in excellent physical health and shape at this time. The healthy food, mountain hiking, and walking into town have transformed our bodies. Tanned and toned, I spend less time thinking about what to wear, what makeup to buy, blow-drying my hair—I have never felt so free and alive. Elated by the beauty of nature that surrounds us, the sounds of the river flowing rapidly over the rocks, and the smell of trees and moist soil, every day is a blessing to be treasured and recalled in the future when I need to bring my mind to a serene, happy place.

Most days remain unplanned, yet every day fills with extraordinary activities and moments. Today, I wake up to a cacophony of bells, run to the window, and see a herd of about fifteen huge brown Swiss cows, decked out with their fanciest and loudest cowbells, being herded down our street by one man, one woman, and a dog. We learn that in the fall the cattle are brought down from the high mountain areas to the warmer, lower pastures and barns. Some smaller herds travel from one field to another on a regular basis for "greener pastures." The field next to our house is occasionally used for grazing a few cows, much to my delight. Holk and Margrith are a little less enthusiastic because the novelty of round-the-clock ringing of the cowbells has worn off.

Well, the cows have come home—and we are still in Switzerland. We'll be here another month for sure, since we have been invited to change our current status as renters to house/dog/cat sitters while Margrith and Holk go on holiday. A month of free rent will be a good thing, and their dog, Lisa, should be fun to take care of. She is a true, well-behaved Swiss dog who loves hiking up the mountains and swimming in the rivers. She is accustomed to walking at around six-thirty in the morning, so certain behavior modifications will be in order, either by the dog or by us.

We enjoy the company of the extraordinary Margrith. She speaks excellent English. She works with Holk at the Subaru dealership every day and maintains their two houses—a beautiful three-bedroom house in Oberried by the Brienzersee, which they own for rental purposes, and of course the three-story Swiss chalet in which we all live. It has been in the family since the early 1900s. They have raised four children and have two grandchildren (with more on the way). Her family owned hotels, so Margrith was raised in that atmosphere and has worked hard all her life. She thrives on being busy. She still has time to meet with her English Club (I have been invited to join her next Thursday) and doesn't hesitate to take a trip to Zurich and Bern for a show or concert. She and Holk have traveled to Subaru conventions in various parts of the world (including the States).

Holk is a gentle, sweet man whose very presence is soothing. He is never without his dog. At home, when Holk is relaxing in a chair, one hand is always petting Lisa. He walks with her to the dealership every day—a few miles into town—comes home at lunchtime with her for Margrith's excellent cooking, and then heads back to the shop. He spends hours training Lisa when he is not working. There is an informal contest among local dog owners involving retrieving sticks. Holk and Lisa win every time—hardly a contest. He will throw no fewer than five sticks while she sits at his side, and on his command she is told to retrieve them all. She never fails. When he demonstrates this for Michael and me, he is typically very quiet and calm—but there is a definite gleam in his eye when Lisa retrieves them once again. When Michael and I take her for walks, she has been guilty of retrieving logs from other folks' woodpiles and bringing them home. A very un-Swiss thing to do! But I'm not going to rat her out.

What a treat it is for us to have our own teachers of Swiss life and have them direct us to the special places of Interlaken and surrounding villages that are not necessarily in the guidebooks. Even though Margrith grew up in neighboring Grindelwald, she gets as much pleasure as we do when she joins us on our outings and relives all the wonders through our eyes. I think we are having an effect on her as well. She is giving serious thought to selling the dealership sooner rather than later, as she wants to spend more time traveling, one of her passions. We're not so sure this is in Holk's plan, but Margrith is quite an independent woman. We've already agreed to swap houses when (or if) we settle down and actually have one to swap. The beauty of traveling vertically instead of horizontally is that we open up opportunities like this, develop relationships with the locals, and truly get into the rhythm of the place. How can this be accomplished if you spend a week or two here and there, frantically trying to see everything?

* * *

One day, Margrith asks us if we'd like to join her for the evening—Holk is going to Germany (about seven hours by train) to visit his father. The nearby town of Brienz is celebrating the seasonal closing of the restaurant on the top of Rothorn Mountain, about 2,600 meters high. The cog-train ride up is free for this event. We arrive in Brienz just in time to hop on one of three special tour trains that hold 300 people each, with sliding windows that open for great viewing. Everyone seems excited and ready for action—if the chorus of unusually excited, sing-song Suisse Deutsche is any indication.

I love the language here—it lifts you up just to hear it. The common greeting in Suisse Deutsche is something like *grüssich, greetse,* or *gruess gott.* Anything of that sort will do, but we must start at the bottom of the vocal scale and end at the top with every word. Then everyone thinks we're Swiss and will readily respond. We never understand the response, but we've got to figure our effort at speaking the language is appreciated.

The train to the restaurant leaves at 7:40 p.m. on the dot. (No surprise here. I'm thinking there is a death penalty for conductors arriving late but have no proof because, to date, it's never happened.) We start snaking up the mountain, through the woods. The fog that has settled in the valley is still thick, and I have no expectations of seeing anything. Quite frankly, I am concerned about staying warm with all the windows wide open. The train whistle toots like crazy, alerting every cow within range, and we climb up quickly with a nice view of the Brienzersee below. The folks close the windows, and we pass through the fog, a few tunnels, and more woods. Some people point at a tree that we pass with an unusual flower hanging on it. Margrith explains that it isn't a flower at all; it is a collection of pacifiers stuck on the tree. There is a tradition here that when a child is ready to give up the little sucker, they can come up here and add it to the bunch—a rite of passage into toddlerhood.

As we chug up the mountain, the forest disappears and the mountains become bare and craggy, with traces of snow on them. About thirty minutes into the ride, the train rises out of the fog. What an eerie and magnificent sight to behold! We look down at a sea of fog with the tops of the mountain ranges jutting out of it. The sun is setting, and the snow on the mountain peaks catches the variety of hues. The moon is rising, and the combination is breathtaking. Margrith is just as excited as we are. At the top, we disembark and take a quick look around before we make haste to the restaurant with its typically cozy wood interior. We select spaghetti Bolognese from the menu. Other selections include ham, a wurst of some sort, *spaetzli,* and *rösti* (shredded potatoes and onions in a pancake style)—a typical Swiss max-cal menu. For dessert we have scrumptious dark chocolate mousse topped with real whipped cream.

After dinner, the local towns have their "oompah" brass bands and vocalists entertain us with honest-to-goodness Swiss yodeling. We are informed that Swiss yodeling is much slower than Austrian yodeling. You can easily start yodeling if you drink *Café Luz,* which is a little coffee dosed with a lot of pear schnapps. So here we are, just days back from the States, perched atop a mountain in the Swiss Alps, becoming experts on yodeling.

※ ※ ※

One of the most obvious differences between the United States and Switzerland is that here people walk everywhere. Informative yellow signs posted throughout town and along the most remote path in the woods tell you how long it takes to get from one place to another on foot. They've got it down to a science—2 *stunde 13 min,* meaning two hours and thirteen minutes. They take into account a timeout for your dog to take a couple of dumps in the woods because everybody has at least one dog. There are strategically located plastic dispensers with baggies for cleaning up after it too. They take into account a short stop on a bench that is located at just the right spot for a view of the lakes or the mountains. We see people of all ages on these trails. One lady we see regularly really blows our mind—she is so hunched-over that the only direction she can possibly look is down at her feet. She walks with two canes, a backpack perched on her hunched back, and yet she walks all over town. Bicycles are a ubiquitous form of transportation. The train system is pristine and easy to figure out. One truly does not need to have a car. But if you do take your vehicle, you get an eyeful of one gorgeous village after another.

There are villages nestled by the lakes; there are villages high up on the mountains. Giessbach, one of our favorites, has an icy waterfall at the top of the mountain that plunges into the Brienzersee with hiking trails alongside and a renovated castle/hotel nestled in the forest. It all conjures up fantasies of romantic trysts, fairy-tale weddings, or just the sheer delight of dropping out for a few glorious days. We've been to Lauterbrunen, Brienze, Spietz, Iseltwald, Thun, and Halbkern, all within a half-hour drive of Interlaken.

We decide to visit the Schilthorn Mountain, well-known for the famous scene from the James Bond movie *On Her Majesty's Secret Service.* They are so proud of this that they have a screening room to watch the pertinent clips from the movie, and we are directed to it as we disembark from the cable car. The mountain is 4,450 meters (14,000 feet) high, and a revolving restaurant on top offers panoramic views. The combination of the view, the altitude, and the lack of oxygen makes us giddy. Michael and I step out of the viewing platform onto the narrow, rocky path, which is the beginning of a steep descent—should you be fool enough to attempt it. A sign posted here shows a woman's high-heeled shoe with a line through it—as if! We venture only as far as the half-dozen large, longhaired mountain goats perched on the rocks ahead of us. The goats begin checking our pockets for food, nudging us dangerously close to the edge of the mountain, so we snap our photos and head back to safer ground.

Midway down the mountain, we get off the cable car in a village called Mürren. We follow a hiking trail that winds gently down through picturesque little villages dotted with wooden chalets and beautifully tended gardens. The sunny, clear, and cool weather provides the perfect day to enjoy a picnic lunch of fresh bread, cheese, fruit, and real Swiss mountain water. The beers will come later in the evening. It's just another typical day in this resplendent countryside.

* * *

Some of the highlights of our time in Switzerland include climbing the Harder Kulm (about 2,800 meters, or 8,500 feet) from Unterseen with Margrith and Holk, about one and a half hours straight up, for a hearty breakfast at the top; hiking around the tiny village of Isenfluh, high up on a mountain, and hearing the tinkling bells worn by the cows as they graze on green, lush pastures; climbing inside the Trümmelbach Falls, where water roars down from the glaciers at a rate of 20,000 liters a second; the cable ride in Grindelwald up the Männlichen and hiking from there with Lisa (our daughter, not the dog) to the Kleine Scheidegg, a high mountain pass below and between the Eiger and Lauberhorn peaks in the Bernese Oberland, one of the most beautiful places in the world; and visiting the Ballenberg Museum, an outdoor museum spread over acres of land, filled with typical farmhouses dating back to the thirteenth century that have been relocated from various cantons in Switzerland to the museum. People in authentic Swiss costumes demonstrate how to weave fabric, make cheese, and bake bread. I even have a chance to test out my skills blowing an Alpenhorn. I surprise everyone and manage to blow out a halfway decent note—I wonder where that came from! We visit Thun, Spietz, and Bern (bear pits and all), where we enjoy the history and architecture.

We are ambassadors of the United States. Sometimes the Swiss shake their heads at us for what they consider to be our national bad behavior. They say, "Shame on you Americans for rejecting the nuclear test ban treaty." They can't understand why we still use hormones in our beef and then insist that the European Union buy it.

"Why are there so many guns in the United States?" they ask. "Why are so many children being shot in the schools?"

We wish we had answers for them. They remind us that America is still young.

Hiking with Margrith and Holk

Lisa visits us in Switzerland

Waiting for cheese to age

Love at first sight

Chapter 9

House-Sitting in Switzerland

Today stretches ahead of me, waiting to be shaped.
And here I am, the sculptor who gets to do the shaping.

—Robert Morrisette

Winter looms over Interlaken, but we still love it here. The mornings and evenings are frosty cold these months of October and November, but most days warm up enough for brisk walks. We had planned to be on our way south by now, but instead we are fulfilling our surrogate parent role for Lisa the dog and Pinot the cat for the next three weeks while our friends/landlords are basking on the beaches of Kuala Lumpur.

We take our pet-sitting responsibilities seriously and try to adhere to the schedule that Holk has left for us. He tells us Lisa must be walked no later than 6:30 a.m. and that we must always take a certain path and throw her stick a certain way. She eats at noon and 6:00 p.m. She gets her fur brushed on Thursday mornings and her teeth flossed every other day. The dog is just as anal—she always goes the same way, stops to have her stick thrown at the same spot each time, and does her stuff in the same appropriately designated area. We just follow along; she makes the job easy for us.

"Always the same," as Holk would say. In spite of being set in his ways, or maybe because of that, we love Holk.

One thing Margrith changed prior to her departure on holiday was Lisa's dog food. A few days after they leave, we finish up the old stuff and start her on the new food. The poor dog has some serious gastronomical distress and is becoming a most offensive houseguest. Yikes, can that dog fart. Something has to be done, and quickly. We have to find the same dog food she had been eating, but I have no idea what brand it is—only that it looks like just like Swiss muesli. We go on our mission into town to our favorite bookstore, where the lady who runs the place has always been helpful. We ask her if she knows of any pet shops in town. Of course there is a pet store just around the corner. We go immediately, and I tell the owner—who speaks English, thank goodness—that we are taking care of the Oertels' dog, and does he—

"Oh, Lisa," he says, interrupting. "How is she doing?"

I am so relieved I nearly plant a kiss on his cheek, but I stop myself just in time because the Swiss limit their greetings to shaking hands. He soon points out the Swiss muesli dog food that Lisa eats. Small towns certainly do have their advantages.

That night, the three of us snuggle together in the flat with no further offensive disturbances—from the dog, at least. What is it about men?

The past month has been filled with social activities as a result of my being an honorary visiting token American of the English Club. It all began when Margrith invited me to join her for one of her weekly meetings, and I have since been invited to participate for the remainder of my stay in Switzerland. The group members started meeting about eight years ago under the tutelage of an instructor to improve their English language skills. The instructor no longer attends, but they continue to meet once a week. It's a perfect excuse to talk about everyday issues, like any other women's group in the world—only Swiss style. It's not in any way comparable to an episode of *Sex in the City*, but I am delighted to be included.

The group is currently comprised of six women: Margrith; Junko, Japanese and married to a Swiss man; Rosemary Papandraou, Swiss and married to a Greek doctor; another Rosemary, British, raised in New Zealand, and married to a Swiss man; Ruth, Swiss and married to the mayor of the small town we all live in (Unterseen); and Maryse Ryter, Swiss, never married, and retired a year ago after practicing family medicine in Unterseen for the past thirty years.

I spend a good bit of time with Maryse. She is in probably in her mid-sixties, brilliant, and interested in everything. She bought a computer a year ago, and I am teaching her what I know about computers, which isn't much. But I have the advantage of knowing all the American techie buzzwords, which I use with great panache. Maryse amazes me. Just this past summer, she backpacked in the Italian Alps for five weeks with her sister, who is a year older than she.

I have to clarify this. "Backpacking as in carrying your tent, clothes, and food supplies on your back?"

She answers, "Yes."

"Like hiking up and down mountains, sleeping in sleeping bags on the ground, and dealing with wild beasts and Italian men?"

"Yes."

Wow! I am so impressed and pleased. I mean, what if I haven't yet reached my peak age and my ability to learn new skills? Is the best yet to come, as Maryse is proving? Further conversation reveals that she has been to Greece and Turkey, has studied in Italy, and speaks several languages. She's a treasure, and we'll continue an e-mail relationship. Michael and I join her for a concert held in a church in Sigriswil, a small village overlooking the Thunersee where the Russian Boys' Choir performs.

On another evening, Maryse, her friend Clara, and I go to a Chopin concert being held in the Farmers School outside of Spiez. The Farmers School is intriguing—it's a two-year program, and the prerequisites for admissions are (i) know how to milk a cow and (ii) have spent three months on an Alp as an apprentice working with cows. The program teaches everything from animal husbandry to making cheese, as well as administrative responsibilities. What's more impressive is that when you graduate, you can actually tell one cow from another! Maryse's sister is also a doctor. She will be retiring this spring and wants to go into this program. The only problem may be finding someone to take care of her house and dog while she is knee-deep in cow shit for three months. Perhaps we can come up with a solution for that.

It's the middle of November, and Margrith and Holk are back from their trip. We have our last fondue dinner together, for now at least, and fill each other in on our respective adventures. Holk is mighty relieved that Lisa is safe and sound and that her schedule was not greatly altered.

Then it snows a couple of inches and, although we have fun romping around in it, it is our cue to pack up and get out of town. Driving up and down the roads in the Swiss Alps with our recently rebuilt, significantly underpowered Subaru will be challenging enough without having to contend with snow. It's nice, though, to have a vehicle to throw all our belongings into and just take off whenever the spirit moves us. We have no set itinerary, but our goal is to be in Tel Aviv by the second week of January. We plan to meet our daughter Rachel's flight and bring her to

Jerusalem so she can begin her spring session at Hebrew University. We have no hotel rooms lined up—we no longer worry about where we'll next rest our heads.

What a delicious sense of freedom. We feel like a couple of teenagers on spring break, always ready for a new adventure. Michael and I have enjoyed the feeling of home over the past few months in our beautiful Swiss chalet and having the opportunity to make friends. I feel enriched and nourished by Switzerland visually, physically, and mentally. But we both feel that there is more to see on our journey, and our time is now.

And so, *auf wiedersehen*, Switzerland ... and *buon giorno*, Italy!

CHAPTER 10

Switzerland through Italy en Route to Israel

A good holiday is one spent among people whose notions of time are vaguer than yours.

—J. B. Priestly

In order to reach Israel, we must take ferryboats that can transport both us and the Subaru. We will drive to Ancona, Italy, take a ferry to the mainland of Greece, and eventually travel back to Paros for a month until we take another ferry from Athens to Israel.

The first day of driving, we cross the Swiss border into Italy. We spend the night in Lake Como, in the northern part of the country. The town wraps around Lake Como, with old cobbled streets, stone buildings and piazzas, and a medieval church that is beautifully lit at night. In contrast to the ancient scene, there are several elegant retail-clothing stores that carry well-known Italian brands of shoes, knit dresses, sweaters, and exquisite men's suits. The Italian people are *trés chic*, even in the most remote little villages. It's the only time that I feel a bit underdressed in my well-worn jeans and boots, fleece shirt, and Gortex jacket, and I begin to think about the nicer clothes I have rotting in storage back in Florida.

The following day, we drive past Milano and Bologna and into Italy's Tuscany region. We eschew the main highways and take the secondary roads that twist and turn up and down the hillsides of the region. Old stone dwellings line the road, and there is little traffic. An almost tangible sense of pride oozes from the Italians—about their architecture, their history, and certainly their food.

We spend the night in a hotel in Pistoia. It's off-season, so we find quite reasonable prices. We stayed there last April when we traveled with John Pack. The host offers us a special drink to welcome us back. My wine is served in a water glass filled to the top; Michael's, in a typical wine glass.

The host says, "This is an old Italian custom. The women get served large glasses so they will get drunk and the men can take advantage of them."

I believe it because that's exactly what happens. But who's complaining? We do, however, manage to go across the street and have a scrumptious dinner at San Jacobi restaurant. Michael has mussel soup and a grilled veal chop. I have a seafood plate of steamed calamari, shrimp, and mussels in a light garlic sauce, with grilled sea bass for the main course. We share a bottle of wine and a salad. Profiteroles and espresso are served for dessert. We stumble across the street, satiated and convinced there must be Italian blood in our ancestry.

The next day, we drive to Cortona, of *Under the Tuscan Sun* fame, and stay for two nights with expatriate friends whom we know from Miami. We tour Cortona on foot, visit some sites of interest, have delicious meals that our friends cook for us, and buy some good wine and olive oil for the road.

* * *

We are all set to head east to Ancona and pick up the ferry to Greece. Only one problem—the gas stations throughout Italy are going on strike tomorrow. Here's where positive attitude comes in again. So, what's the worst that can happen? Get stuck in Italy? Maybe that's the good news. The food alone is to die for, and after Switzerland, where their best-known food is the *wurst*, we are savoring the height of gastronomical delights. We know we can't make it to Ancona on one tank of gas, since our Subaru only holds about three pints. We consult a book that our friends have on bed-and-breakfasts in Italy and select Agriturismo Malvarina, Capodacqua di Assisi. It is en route, with reasonable off-season rates. We call and book for three nights, figuring that will get us through until the gas stations reopen.

After a few hours of driving, we enter the region of Umbria and arrive in Assisi. It is dark and cold by now, but we spot the signs for Malvarina and drive up a winding unlit road to a beautiful old farmhouse. We knock on the door, and Maria comes out of the kitchen wearing a long wool skirt with her white apron over it. She looks elegant. She speaks no English but rings up her son, Claudio, to come take care of us. While we wait for him, I pick up their brochure and read that Maria is a gourmet cook and has been written up in *Bon Apetit* and featured on CNN. When Claudio arrives, he asks if we will be joining the group for a family-style dinner tonight. *Are you kidding?* We jump on that offer like bums on a bologna sandwich.

An hour later, we are sitting with a group of fourteen people— Italians from different regions who come for Maria's famous dinners, two couples from Chicago, and a young Japanese woman traveling by herself. The dining room is in a separate building, decorated with antiques and warm and cozy from the heat generated by a huge fireplace glowing with hot coals.

The dinner guests gather around while our host toasts Tuscan bread over the grill in the fireplace. Once it is perfect, he removes it from the grill and rubs it with a cut clove of garlic, then sprinkles on a deep-green olive oil made from the olives grown on the farm at Malvarina.

"You must use the ring finger to pat down the olive oil," he explains to us while ceremoniously pouring a few drops on the toast and patting it. "No other finger produces the same results." He then adds a light sprinkling of salt. The result is, indeed, perfection. Adding *pomodoro* sauce to it is optional, but the flavor of the olive oil is so wondrously subtle, it seems a shame to hide it beneath sauce. We've never had bruschetta as heavenly as this.

This becomes our nightly ritual. We all sit at one large table where pitchers of red wine sit in front of every other person. The wine is also a product of the farm and makes the perfect complement to the dinners. The food is brought to the table—lots of it. There is no fanfare about it and no cute little printed menus, so we don't know the names of the particular dishes that we are enjoying so much. Most of the dishes are Maria's specialties.

The First Big Night

> Bruschetta *pomodoro* (described above)
> Lentil soup
> Fish and *riso* (rice) salad (served cold, interesting texture)
> Spaghetti with lentil sauce (Maria's pastas are unlike anything
> I've ever eaten; the sauces are rich and flavorful)

Riso with Parmesan and grilled veggies (served hot)
Chicken with herbs grilled over hot coals in the fireplace
Green salad with vinaigrette
White heart of beets (fennel to us) with cheese (served hot)
Eggplant with tomato sauce
Strudel-type pastry with pear and raspberry marmalade
Rice pastry à la Maria (like a rice pudding donut)
Espresso
Limoncello (liquor made from fresh lemons; supposedly a good digestive, and God knows we need one by now)

Another Big Night

Bruschetta (of course)
Vegetable soup—fresh herbs and light broth
Thinly sliced salami served with chopped parsley in olive oil
Tagliatelle with light tomato sauce and mushrooms
Grilled mushrooms (over the fire)
Mashed potatoes with roasted pork chunks in a sauce (Michael's favorite)
Green salad with vinaigrette
Thick vanilla cream pudding with whipped cream and cherries
Espresso
Nocino (liquor made from walnuts; also a good digestive)

The Last Big Night

Bruschetta (so good; must be the ring finger)
Faro (spelt) with Parmesan and *pomodoro* (my favorite)
Linguini with tomato and cheese sauce
Roast pork
Swiss chard
Baby zucchini and tomatoes
Green salad with vinaigrette
Italian pastry with paper-thin cooked apples, decorated with local pomegranate seeds and orange slices
Espresso and limoncello and/or nocino

Dinners begin at 8:30 and wind down around 11:00. Conversations are limited due to all the different languages and perhaps because everyone is busy eating. The food is served promptly, and there is not much waiting between courses. All in all, it is perfection.

All this indulging calls for some serious walking. During the day, we drive about five minutes into Assisi and walk. We discover that we will be leaving just before the reopening of St. Francis Basilica.

A few days after we leave Italy, we read an article in the *International Herald* about Assisi:

> When a powerful earthquake crushed the vaulted ceiling of the St. Francis Basilica two years ago, the damage to priceless thirteenth and fourteenth century frescoes was so devastating that it overshadowed the loss of eleven lives and many thousands of homes. The Basilica, one of the most revered shrines in the Roman Catholic Church, will be fully reopened next Sunday. The extraordinary restoration of the early Renaissance masterpiece was so speedy and efficient that it has been dubbed "the miracle of Assisi." Unfortunately there were over 40,000 people left homeless, and more than 10,000 of them are still living in tin containers, 375-square-foot metal boxes.

Interesting priorities, but the Italians do take the preservation of their history seriously. They are truly masters of reconstruction, and there were projects throughout the country with "Jubilee 2000" signs, which indicated that these are state-funded for reconstruction.

We also visit and fall in love with Spello, another medieval hill town a few minutes away, where we enjoy meandering through the variety of small shops selling wines, salami of all kinds, and an abundance of religious icons. These villages are built high up on the hills for protection from their enemies, and they have gorgeous views of the lush valleys surrounding them. In the distance, I can see the snowcapped Dolomites. The weather is brisk and clear, and we are energized and in high spirits.

The morning after we arrive in Malvarina, someone mentions in passing that the gas strike is over—only one day after it began. This is the way it is in Italy. Nobody gets uptight for too long, and life goes on.

Four days later, we head out of Assisi several pounds heavier than when we arrived. We drive to Ancona, go straight to the port, and purchase our ferry tickets for Igoumenitsa, Greece. Later that evening, we drive our Subaru onto the ferry amidst 10,000 huge trucks, and I am sure the ferry is going to sink under all the weight. We wisely reserved a cabin, which, to our delight and utter surprise, is comfortable and has a bathroom and shower. We pop the cork on one of our Italian wines, feast on salami and cheese, and sleep for most of the fifteen-hour trip.

Arrivederci, Italy.

CHAPTER 11

Mainland Greece

> To feel at home, stay at home. A foreign country is not designed to make you comfortable … It's designed to make its own people comfortable.
>
> —Clifton Fadiman

We drive off our ferry in Igoumenitsa—no customs, no checkpoints—onto the east coast of the Greek mainland. We are excited to see this storied part of the country, to absorb as much of the culture and history as we possibly can, and driving through it is at least a beginning. There is nothing much to see in Igoumenitsa, which basically appears to be a port city full of travel agencies and banks, so we keep going until we come to Ioannina. The countryside from the coast eastward is mountainous and rugged, with steep ranges and hairpin turns. We chug up in second gear for the most part; the landscape tests both our Subaru and Michael's driving. Fortunately, there is little traffic because few people live in this part of the country. We pass scattered homes and farms en route, but few other signs of habitation. The leaves change hue on the trees, and this provides some color to an otherwise bleak vista. We stay overnight in Ioannina and enjoy a walk in the historical town center. We're back to *gyros, souvlaki,* and Greek salad.

The following day we go to Meteora, which Michael says is as spectacular as he remembered it from his visit thirty years ago. We go into one of the monasteries perched atop the huge, precipitously steep rocks. It fills me with awe and wonder. Astonishingly tall stone blocks are heaped one on top of one another in a column with monasteries on top and trees growing around them. We fall into step with a priest visiting from Romania, who says, "This could only come from God."

We continue farther east across the mainland until the road finally turns south toward Delphi and, ultimately, Athens. We drive through more mountain ranges with wide valleys separating them. We pass through a couple of pretty villages—those that have a little tourist business—and some really strange ones that seem to have developed haphazardly, without a plan. The main highway—the only one, and a paltry one at that—goes directly through these places, twisting and turning for a few blocks until it straightens out again. Mostly, the drive is through empty country. Greece's population is only about 11 million— half of whom live in Athens.

We pass a campsite in the midst of a muddy, barren field where poor, ragged people live in rigged-up tents only a few meters from a large dump where garbage burns and the smoke blows directly into the campsite. We learn that this is an Albanian refugee camp. There are about a hundred families living in these horrible conditions. Until this moment, a refugee camp was something we'd only read about; it didn't have much meaning. Now it will be hard to forget.

As we continue south through the middle of the country to Delphi, located high up on the spur of Mount Parnassus, we can see the Gulf of Corinth in the distance. We wander along the empty streets of Delphi with no sign of the famed Oracle. It is said that when Zeus sought to find the center of Grandmother Earth (or Gaia), he sent two eagles flying from the eastern and western extremities. The paths of the eagles crossed over Delphi, where the *omphalos*, or navel of Gaia, was found. The frosty weather convinces us it is time to head to warmer climes.

We arrive in Athens and then the port of Piraeus. It was worthwhile to tour the mainland of Greece, but once in a lifetime is enough. We drive our little Subaru onto the ferry and look forward to returning to our beloved island of Paros.

CHAPTER 12

Back to Paros

Be like a very small joyous child, living gloriously in the ever-present NOW, without a single worry or concern about even the next moment of time.

—Eileen Caddy

It is Thanksgiving, and we are happy to be back on our wonderful little island of Paros. John Pack lined up a beautiful villa for us for just US$150 a month. It's about twenty feet from the Aegean Sea, just outside of the main town of Parikia in a place called Agia Irini. It's spacious, almost new, and white with blue shutters (okay, every house in Greece is white with blue shutters). It came fully furnished and offers a laundry service, a fireplace, a full kitchen, two bedrooms, three porches, and six cats. The owner and developer, Kostas, is warm and friendly, and just about every day he asks us to let him know if there is anything at all we need. A little central heating would be just fine and dandy—but alas, there's no point in asking. I know it would make him feel bad, and we are managing just fine with three space heaters, the oven, and the fireplace going full blast. We'll stay here until after the holidays.

Most folks on the island at this time of the year are the native Parians and a few expatriates. The weather ranges from the midsixties down to the forties at night, too cold for the restaurants to set up their tables outdoors, and the island has a different feel to it than during the spring and summer seasons. It's barren, stark, and less populated. New faces stand out and are a topic of discussion. It's fun for us, though, because we met quite a few people during our last stay of five months, and walking through town to do our errands becomes a social outing.

I almost can't believe how quickly time passes. What on earth do we do all day? It's amazing how the day can fill up with the most mundane of missions. Starting with a leisurely cup of coffee on the sunny south patio, rereading yesterday's newspaper, listening to one of our CDs (classical music in the morning), then a brisk shower (if we're feeling brave), and dressing. By about nine or nine-thirty in the morning, it's time for breakfast, outdoors if it's warm enough. Breakfast is fruit (in this season, tangerines grow on the island and are sweet, juicy, and seedless) and plain yogurt with locally harvested honey, or eggs and fresh-baked bread with fresh orange juice. Next, we compile a list of things we simply must do. Our list is never longer than two or three items, but somehow having a list adds a sense of mission to our meanderings. There's the daily trip to the fresh veggie and fruit market, as well as the bakery. Sometimes we are expecting a piece of mail, so going to the post office becomes an item on our list. Just about every day, we go to the Wired Café to do our web surfing and e-mailing. The Wired Café has an ISP connection, so we just insert the PC card into our laptop and we're able to connect. They serve coffee and play some good music. It's a nice way to take care of business. We have no phone line at the villa, so it also becomes an important item on our "mission" list. After one-thirty in the afternoon, the ferry brings in the *International Herald Tribune*, so we pick up the paper.

By now, we've worked up a huge appetite and will either eat in town or drive back to our villa for lunch. We read the paper and our books and write letters. Michael reviews the status of the stock market to determine our level of solvency. Then it's time for a siesta. We go for a long walk in the mountains or take a drive to another part of the island and hike there. On a big day, we may pack a picnic lunch and head off to neighboring Antiparos or Naxos. Some days, however, are so slow that taking our garbage down the road to the dumpster is the main event.

Each evening, we prepare for our ritual of watching the sunset. We'll have an *aperitif* on the front porch and listen to Pavarotti to set the mood. Before we know it, it's time for dinner. We either join one of our friends for a bite to eat in town or fix up dinner at home. After dinner, it's time to kick back and relax after another hard day—that is, after another glorious, it's-good-to-be-alive kind of day. My inbred Jewish guilt may rear up anytime and say, "Enough of all this fun and leisure."

But I'm going to ride this wave as long as I can and worry about running aground some other time. We're loving life and each other.

* * *

Meanwhile, in Paros, everyone is a weatherman. I guess there are not a lot of things to worry about, so the main topic of discussion is from which direction the wind blows. The wind direction tells everything—air temperatures, sun or rain, if the fish are biting, ferry schedules (which for us mean newspaper or no newspaper), good olive-picking weather, and odd behavior by animals. Even man's behavior is associated with certain winds. (Oh yes, that is a fact. Ill winds have served as a valid legal excuse for murder of a spouse.) And one more thing—whether or not you can light your fireplace! A south wind means smoke in your face. You can understand the importance of wind direction on this island and the need for endless discussion.

And while wind is the topic of conversation among Parians, the bathrooms are what get us foreigners talking. They don't make any sense whatsoever. For example, the showerheads are handheld nozzles with weak sprays and no place to hook them while you attempt to wet your body. So, while soaping yourself, you have to hold the nozzle between your legs or under an arm or just let the thing hang. In any case, there's a 100 percent chance you'll spray the entire bathroom because there are no shower curtains. Thus, the whole bathroom becomes the shower. To the designers' credit, there are drains in the floor to handle the flood. Planning ahead is critical here—putting the dry towels outside the bathroom, along with the toilet paper, as well as all your clothes. So basically, there's a lot of prancing around the house stark-naked and dripping wet, and we've been freezing our asses off because it's winter and the house is not heated. But you can't beat the price. Also, several days after we arrive, we are informed that it is a good idea to shut off the hot water heater, which is located in the bathroom/shower, so that we don't get electrocuted whilst showering! Showering every day seems to be an exclusively American thing. Now I know why.

While we are on the subject of bathrooms, here's another thing I don't understand: the toilet bowls. They are constructed in the most ridiculous fashion. I mean, one has no choice but to examine what one has just deposited. The bowl is shaped so that the water is hidden toward the back or the front of the bowl (never where your droppings land) and only holds about a thimbleful of water in any case. But not to worry, every bathroom comes complete with a toilet brush.

The Greek plumbing system cannot handle toilet paper, so they compensate with a sophisticated method of placing a wastebasket next to the bowl. Having gotten that far, it's time to flush. There are a variety of pull or push or pump devices, usually well-hidden, but any kind is better than no kind. Michael and I had been traveling on the mainland of Greece for about three days when we pulled into a gas station and I had to use the bathroom. Given the choice, I much prefer to use the great outdoors than a public bathroom in Greece. But we needed to fill up with petrol, so I figured I'd take advantage of the opportunity. Michael walked with me around to the back of the station to where we were told the WC was.

I opened the door and said, "Hey, this one's really good!"

To which Michael said, "Jean, I think you've been on the road too long."

As I squatted over the bowl because there was no toilet seat and took a better look around, I started laughing so hard it was nearly a disaster. It's just that I was so darn glad that this bathroom had a toilet bowl instead of what I call "treadmills," which are places to plant your feet while you squat over a hole that leads God knows where. I hate those treadmills, especially if I'm wearing a backpack that could throw my balance off, with my jeans down to my ankles and my butt hanging out. What could be worse than to lose my balance and touch anything with any part of my body? As I continued to look around, I saw that the sink had water trickling down and so much rust on it that Apollo himself might have used it—but at least there was a sink, and there was soap, which was greatly appreciated. There was no toilet paper, but I'd grown accustomed to carrying it with me at all times, and there was a wastebasket, which was not overflowing. The flushing device was an unraveled wire hanger coming down from the ceiling—but it flushed! All in all, I was not wrong in my enthusiasm. This WC was A-OK with me.

* * *

Back in town, I think the Wired Café could be the scene for a TV series, something like "The Expatriate Games." We walk in and see several people working on computers, including Karen, our Scottish friend who runs Meltemi Bar; a few of John Pack's art students, whom we met at his Thanksgiving dinner; Marta and Nicolas, the couple that owns the Wired; and Don the sculptor, who is still trying to make enough money to get off the island and back to California (he's been here four and a half years) and still wearing the same well-worn Rollerblades. We pick up Martien's e-mail message asking us if we can take care of Koita, the wonderful dog whom we fell in love with on our last stay on Paros. We use Nicolas's phone to contact Martien, but there is no answer.

Karen perks up and says, "I just saw him at Remezzo Café."

Then Marta chimes in, "No, he has left there. We just saw him right up the street from here."

Soon, everyone is in on the discussion of where Martien might be. We tell the group that we are going to care for his dog while he goes to Athens to visit a sick friend. News travels fast here on Paros, and everyone already knows that he is leaving shortly. We finally get Martien on his cell phone and ease his concern about the dog. He says he'll leave word with Karen at Meltemi to let us know when he's coming back, since we have no phone at home. So, having straightened all that out, we go back to typing our various e-mails.

Apart from the time spent on e-mails and the like, cooking is one of my favorite pastimes, and it's really taken on an international flair. I have herbs from Provence, chili from Turkey, soups from Switzerland, olive oil from Italy, our favorite cookies from France, and the wine and olives from the island here. I am in the midst of a wild cooking spree, using my favorite seasonings, which I have schlepped all over the world. But dammit, I left my paprika in Switzerland!

Our six-week layover has passed so quickly. We have enjoyed renewing our friendships and experiencing the winter season, and we can now say we've seen all four seasons of Paros. I'm sad to say good-bye but ready for the next adventure. We're booked on ferryboats from here to Haifa—next year in Jerusalem.

Martien, our Paros neighbor

Koita hangin' with us

CHAPTER 13

Journey to Israel

Travel is the opposite of a holiday. It is about enlightenment and, at its best, is a form of disappearance … much of futurology is idle speculation. We cannot know what the world will look like 100 years from now, but travel is a human imperative. Enlightenment will always involve the poetry of departures.

—Paul Theroux

Michael and I are sitting in our cabin on the ferryboat heading from Athens to Haifa, Israel. The seas are rough, and the wind is blowing like hell. We are doing some pretty serious rocking and rolling, but we are wearing sea bands on our wrists—acupressure theory in action—that help prevent seasickness. We've secured our belongings in the cabin so they aren't flying all over the place, and we are managing reasonably well—a lot better than folks who don't have cabins or sea bands.

We leave Athens the evening of January 3, 2000, in the midst of a northern front, complete with wind and light snow. During the night there are heavy seas. I am sliding with the motion of the boat, from the head of the bed to the foot and back again, and I get pretty good at holding onto the blankets and pillow during the ride. What's more, the engines vibrate like crazy, so in general it's rather an awful experience.

At least we have our own facilities, such as they are. We have the typical Greek bathroom/shower combo—we finally figure out that the sink faucet snakes out and becomes the showerhead. The water in the toilet bowl sloshes around in accordance with the swells in the seas, flooding the bathroom floor and adding to the overall ambiance. Suffice it to say, this ain't *The Love Boat*.

It's disconcerting that so far all the announcements have been only in Greek. When we've been fortunate enough to find someone who can translate at least a portion of the announcements for us, they've been about when the restaurant or the duty-free shop is open. We have missed every meal time, and one night we ate with the kitchen staff, who took pity on us. If there is an emergency and they announce, "Man the lifeboats!" we'll undoubtedly head straight for the restaurant.

When we wake up, the boat is stopped. I had a feeling that we'd be in trouble as soon as I found out the name of our ship is *Poseidon*. We step out of our cabin and peer through the nearest porthole and, thank goodness, we are docked, not drifting out in the middle of the sea. Nobody is around, neither crew nor passenger. We finally notice a sign with nine o'clock written on it. We figure it means if a passenger exits the boat, he should return to it by that time. We have just enough time to get off the boat, buy a couple of fresh loaves of bread (we are starving), withdraw a few more drachmas from the ATM (in case we need to bribe the cooks to give us some food), and make it back in time to head out to sea once again. Evidently, this is a scheduled two-hour stop on the island of Patmos, but who knew?

Late in the afternoon, we reach the Greek Island of Rhodes and are scheduled to have another three-hour stop here. The sea is choppy, and the conditions at the dock are so bad that the captain has us wait until he decides it is safe enough to remain docked, or we will have to immediately go back out to sea. Thankfully, he gives us the go-ahead, and as we walk down the ramp of the ship we nearly blow away. We head into Old Town, just a few blocks from the harbor. It is dark and cold and most of the stores are closed, but we find a cozy little restaurant and enjoy a tasty dinner and a brisk walk back to the ship. The crew is standing by to assist us individually up the sea-splashed gangplank, which is rising and falling with the swells of the sea. We have to time the waves so the ramp is not too steeply inclined, and at just the right moment we need to literally run up the ramp to get on board the ferry.

We survive a second night of rough seas, and the next morning the ferry docks for a few hours on the Greek part of Cyprus. We have lunch in the Old City, and it feels good to be on land and to take a long walk along the promenade. This is not the way to visit a place, and I cannot get the feel of it in such a short time. We get back on the ferry for one last night's passage.

Our *Poseidon*

CHAPTER 14

Living in Jerusalem

Travel is fatal to prejudice, bigotry, and narrow-
mindedness, and many of our people need it sorely on
these accounts. Broad, wholesome, charitable views of
men and things cannot be acquired by vegetating in one
little corner of the earth all one's lifetime.

—Mark Twain

Shalom, shalom. We've made it to Haifa. We pull into the port at
6:30 in the morning just in time to see the sun rising behind the soft
hills of Israel. Michael and I stand on the deck in eager anticipation
of our forthcoming adventure. We take a moment or two to reflect on
what it must have been like to enter this country as a refugee, and it is
a poignant feeling for us.

Driving off the ferry in our vehicle, we are told to follow a lead
driver to customs. The security people are all young, attractive, and ever
so serious. Fortunately, we are first in line and make our way through
customs without a problem. Even so, it is a two-hour process.

They ask us, "What countries have you been in over the past few
months? Have you had your car serviced within the last couple of
weeks?" I presume in case some contraband has been placed in it. "Did
anyone know you were coming to Israel? Where are you staying, and
for how long?"

They ask if we have pictures of our children, and then the
authorities are satisfied at last. Our passports are stamped, and they
give us temporary registration for the car. We do not have to unload or
unpack any suitcases, although we notice several people are asked to
do so. The gate is opened for us, we pass two more checkpoints with

soldiers carrying Uzis, and we are released to enter Israel on our own. I have mixed feelings about the whole experience. I am glad they are being cautious, but at the same time it instills paranoia the moment you land—and that feeling persists.

We decide to head straight for Jerusalem to a bed-and-breakfast we select from our *Lonely Planet*. First, we need shekels, gas, and food. We find a gas station and are able to accomplish all this. We change dollars for NIS, which stands for New Israeli Shekel, currently four shekels to the dollar, and the station serves some home-cooked stuff at its food counter. Thus, my first experience with Israeli food is at a gas station … and it is delicious. We have a breakfast dish of eggs cooked in a tomato sauce and put inside a pocket cut into pita bread. Most Israeli food is stuffed into the pita, much like the Greek *gyros*.

Well satiated, gassed up, and with a few shekels in our pockets, we are on our merry way. We drive along the coast heading south from Haifa to Tel Aviv, following the major highway. We skirt around Tel Aviv and head due east toward our destination, Jerusalem, and about an hour later we arrive. Our directions to the B and B are sketchy, at best, but we sense that we are close. Stopping to ask for directions is an experience. Arabs and Jews alike cannot give directions in Jerusalem. In all fairness, it's difficult because the street names change with each block, the highways have no names at all, and some of the roads are not yet on any map. In fact, there are some whole villages in Jerusalem that are not on the map, so navigating is quite a challenge. And, of course, the signs are all in Hebrew. An Israeli tells us that there are two things you should not do—one is to ask for directions, and the second is to follow them.

We have been up since dawn after days on a choppy sea. We have been thoroughly interrogated, have driven for hours, and we are now going in circles trying to find our B and B. Finally, I get out of the car at the Hyatt and beg a taxi driver to lead us to the proper street. He speaks English and says, "No, no, no. You are so close—you don't need a taxi. Just turn left, then right, then another right, then bear to the left, cross over at the light, go left, and then you are there. Easy!"

I repeat his directions, run back to the car, write down verbatim what he said, and at last we find it. It is our first miracle in the holy city.

The B and B is bright, comfy, and has a shower with a shower curtain. A good beginning is at hand. Our host and hostess are from

France, and they are helpful in giving us information. We are staying here for a week, and as luck would have it, they have a two-bedroom furnished apartment available for two months just a couple of blocks away—also in the French Hill area. Jerusalem is the heart of this country. It's sure to be a worthy experience for at least two months.

The day after we arrive, we take the Zion tour—a four-hour walking tour of the Old City. Our guide is also a geography teacher; he's chock full of information, enthusiasm, and fun. We begin to better understand and appreciate the history of the Holy Land. As it turns out, it's the last day of Ramadan, the holiest of Muslim holidays, and there are about 400,000 Arabs in the Old City to pray to Allah. It is also the Greek Orthodox holiday of the Epiphany, so the Holy Sepulcher is the site of hundreds of Christians on their pilgrimage. Boris Yeltsin is here to pray for a little help also. The Sabbath is getting close, so the Jews are home preparing for that. Fortunately our guide does not desert us and in fact steers us to a wonderful Arab restaurant in the Old City, which is open today.

A few days later, we drive east to the Dead Sea. As soon as we descend from the top of the hills of Jerusalem, everything changes dramatically. The weather is warmer; the landscape is arid, filled with Bedouin camps tucked into the hillsides of the barren, sandy canyons. It's absolutely monochromatic, a stark contrast against the blue sky.

Within twenty minutes of leaving Jerusalem, we're at the Dead Sea. Calm blue waters meet the rocky, desert-brown coastline. No birds fly overhead. Fish can't survive in the water's thirty percent salt concentration; regular seawater contains only four percent. Some white chunks of salt float around, and to the east are the mountains and canyons of Jordan in shades of beige and pastels. It looks like one of those sand paintings made in a jar by pouring in different colored grains.

We time it perfectly on our first outing and catch the sunset's reflection off the canyons. I've never seen anything like this in my life. I want to don the *Lawrence of Arabia* white robe and go riding on a stallion through the dunes. We don't go swimming—the weather is sunny but a little cool, and quite frankly the water feels slimy. Apparently, the muddy bottom is full of minerals and magical stuff that they sell all over Israel for a lot of shekels, but it doesn't look appealing, so we pass on it for now. We promise to complete the ultimate Israeli cliché before we leave—float on our backs while reading the newspaper in the Dead Sea.

As planned, we pick up our daughter, Rachel, at Ben Gurion airport in Tel Aviv four days after we arrive. The following day we go to Hebrew University to register her for the semester and set up her dorm room. As seems typical, only minimal information has been provided to the students, orientation is scheduled three days after classes begin, there are no directional signs on campus, and generally nothing is easy.

Days later, Michael asks a tour guide, "Why does government make it so difficult for people to find their way around?"

"It's not easy being a Jew," she says.

Suffering is mandatory. But we accomplish the deed, and Rachel is unfazed by the whole thing. Her roommate is bright, spunky, and speaks some Hebrew. There are about 400 students in the International Program.

One of Rachel's first comments is, "Everyone's Jewish!"

We enjoy having some of her friends over, and they laugh about how they all look like each other and almost everyone has run into someone they know from back home. How great for us to be able to share in the fun and excitement with our daughter. This town is made for young people, and Rachel is the perfect age for getting the most out of this experience.

After being in Israel for a couple of weeks, I'm starting to get the hang of it. There is a lot to absorb. It's a challenge with many contrasts. For example, our *Lonely Planet* guidebook says, "Israelis exhibit near-suicidal tendencies once behind the wheel." Of course, the bad news is they'll take you with them. The drivers are incredibly rude too. The instant a traffic light turns green, they'll hit their horn for you to move. It happens every time. Or they'll squeeze you into a barrier, and curse at you if you hesitate for one second while trying to read one of the rare street signs.

Outside their cars, it's a different story. Most people we've met take the time to chat with us. They are helpful and have a great love for their country. It's infectious. They have the universal "Jewish humor," and Michael, particularly, feels right at home. The main language is Hebrew, of course. Most signs are in Hebrew, Arabic, and occasionally English. Almost everyone speaks English and probably one or two other languages as well. The most amazing thing is being Jewish and being in the majority. It's a good feeling.

My mother and grandfather fled Vienna in 1939 and came to the United States when my mother was eighteen. Growing up, my sister and I were told to keep our religion to ourselves. I remember that I was given a necklace, a small Jewish star on a thin gold chain, as a gift from a friend when I was about twelve years old, and I wasn't allowed to wear it. Mom was afraid, understandably. Now here I am, in Israel, where the majority of the population is Jewish. I didn't think I would feel comfortable in Israel because of my lack of Jewish education, but it doesn't seem to matter. Being born Jewish is enough.

Still, we are unaccustomed to the soldiers with machine guns who patrol the city and the highway checkpoints with soldiers in Army jeeps mounted with artillery. My backpack is checked each time that I go to the supermarket or the mall. The Arabs we have any contact with (vendors, mostly) are friendly and easy to chat with. In fact, our hostess told us that if we want to hire a taxi to go to some of the sites around Jerusalem, we should go to the Damascus Gate and get an Arab driver versus an Israeli driver. They're much cheaper and will be pleased to be of service. One day, there is a bomb scare, so traffic is diverted from one of the main highways for a couple of hours, but no one seems concerned about it. Bomb scares are fairly common.

Hiking through Ein Gedi, an oasis in the midst of the arid, rocky canyons alongside the Dead Sea, leaves us inspired. The Tower of David Museum, guided by a Brit who is a brilliant historian, reminds us of all we have left to learn here. The Chagall windows in the synagogue of the Hadassah Hospital impress us with their beauty. We just don't know what to expect next.

One of our favorite activities is shopping at Mahane Yehuda, a huge outdoor market just west of the Old City of Jerusalem. The stalls that line the streets are laden with all manner of fruits, vegetables, pickles, olives, cheeses, and Middle Eastern foods such as humus, tabouli, and a flavorful eggplant-and-tomato salad mixture that goes well with just about everything. Their baba ghanoush is the best I've ever had, a little sweeter-tasting than in the States. There are chicken and meat stalls, and fish so fresh they have to be beaten into submission before they can be wrapped. There is plenty of fresh, warm pita bread (though their bagels are nothing special), great oranges and other citrus, and fresh vegetables, depending on what's in season. You can find some good pastries, great nuts, and tons of dried fruit that cost very little. We admire the beautifully displayed varieties of spices in the market too.

We buy fresh bread, fruits, veggies, nuts, fish, salads, olives, and a variety of wonderful spices and spend less than US$40. The supermarkets are two or three times more expensive and not as good, so virtually everyone does their shopping here. The outdoor market is crowded and great for people watching too.

The Mahane Yehuda has falafel stands and shawarma (a pita bread stuffed with chicken or lamb, humus, salads, and French fries), and pizza places, but the restaurants are gathered in the Old City or on Ben Yehuda, or in some of the expensive hotels. Many families prefer to have their Sabbath dinners together at home and don't often go out to eat. It's expensive. We've eaten mostly at home, although we plan to try a few places we've been told are pretty good.

We still have to go to the supermarket for a few items. Imagine a store full of hungry Jewish people, all trying to get their shopping done before the Sabbath. Particularly dangerous are the old ladies with canes. Back in the States, the Jewish food in a supermarket is reserved to one small section of one aisle, if that. Here, it's all Jewish food mixed with Middle Eastern. What a blast! The deli department is huge, with various selections of prepared foods and salads for the ease of takeout meals. The labels are in Hebrew, but with pictures, you can figure it out. Cooking instructions are often in Hebrew only, but most people speak English and will translate for you if you ask them.

I am shocked, however, at the way everyone samples the food. Going past the dried fruit? Try a date, an apricot, a prune, and a handful of raisins, why don't you? Nuts? Are you kidding? You *have* to taste the nuts. Pickles, olives, and salami? Can't buy without trying. Is the bread fresh? Open up a package and taste it. It is considered acceptable behavior here. It's so outside my cultural norm that I just can't wrap my mind around it. Meanwhile, Michael dives in for a full meal. I don't know—maybe he has the right idea. After all, we're paying exorbitant prices, most likely because half the groceries are eaten before they get to the checkout. It's Friday, and by two o'clock in the afternoon, everything shuts down for the Sabbath. The weekend is Friday and Saturday. Sunday is the beginning of a new week.

We've seen some unexpected things in Jerusalem. The *hamsin* is a dust storm that occurs about fifty days out of the year. The wind picks up the desert sand and blasts right through you, leaving a one-inch layer of dirt on everything (we couldn't discern the white and blue racing stripes on our Subaru minibus). A horse eating shawarma, hitched to a beat-up old buggy parked outside the Damascus Gate of the Old City, had us smiling in wonder. Also, the structures in Jerusalem are made out of the local rock, which creates a sort of monochrome vista with few breaks other than the green trees, which are laboriously and lovingly planted in the rocky soil. How vastly different it is from the Swiss countryside, with its profusion of flowers, green fields, wooden chalets, and my favorite Swiss cows.

I'm beginning to understand that it's beneath this exterior that the beauty lies. All the secrets are within, and it takes those who are determined and persistent to discover them. History is alive here.

Mahani Yehuda market, Shofar so good!

Old City of Jerusalem

The market, spices galore

Michael shopping

CHAPTER 15

Travels in Israel and Jordan

If you reject the food, ignore the customs, fear the religion, and avoid the people, you might better stay at home.

—James Michener

Most people with whom we've had day-to-day dealings have been pleasant, particularly our landlady, Marie-Helene. She says it takes about three or four years of living here to understand the culture and to be accepted. A big part of the acceptance is your ability to speak Hebrew. We haven't encountered too many Israelis on a more personal basis, so it is difficult to judge. We've encountered some rude, pushy people who have no patience; they don't respect lines and barge right in front of you. We just barge right back in. It is the local custom. I suppose if they were meek and subdued, there would be no Israel.

Here in Jerusalem, the Old Testament is alive and much a part of peoples' lives and thinking. For example, the archeological finds at the digs continuously uncover evidence of history that is specifically referred to in the Bible. The Dead Sea Scrolls, which we saw on display at the Israeli Museum, validate the authenticity of the Torah. So here in Jerusalem, the Bible is not just a tale that's been passed along for 6,000 years. It is real, and there are periodic updates. It's different from anything we've experienced in the United States. Although I do not feel part of this, I find it absolutely fascinating. I am enjoying the experience, and I am learning.

Still, I am an outsider—unless I make the commitment to become an Israeli, I will remain an outsider. The prevailing philosophy is that if someone is a Jew, they should become an Israeli. We've driven through the ultra-Orthodox Jewish sections in Jerusalem, where a woman would be ostracized if she were to walk around in pants and without her head covered. If we were to drive through this section on the Sabbath, we would risk getting stones thrown at our car. The various ultra-Orthodox groups don't even get along with each other, and they argue over interpretations of the Torah to the point where they will not associate with each other (let alone with the nonreligious Jews).

In addition to the French Hill colony of Jerusalem, where we are currently renting a little apartment, there is also a German Colony, an American Colony, and a Russian compound that has a huge, beautiful cathedral and lots of bars. It is located right next to Ben Yehuda, an area loaded with stores, restaurants, and many more bars. It is the hot spot for the hundreds of young people who flock here every night, including our Rachel. It's fun and lively, a welcome relief from the intense and sometimes oppressive feeling in the rest of Jerusalem. There are Arab areas interspersed throughout. Some are Catholic; others are Palestinians who remained here after the Six-Day War. Some chose to become Israeli citizens; others did not.

After graduating high school, the Israeli students are inducted into the army. This is not optional. The women are in for two years, and the men for three years. They have several interviews to determine which branch of the military they will serve in.

Our landlady advises us to close the blinds at night. Over dinner, we hear machine-gun fire echo in the background, followed by police sirens. When entering the parking lot at the mall, army officers stop each car and ask questions: "What is your name? Are you visiting?" They look inside your car and under it with a device to check for bombs. Security is intensified when there is an alert—a threat from the Lebanese, Iranians, Palestinians, Syrians, or all of them at once. I guess it's for our own good, but it's a weird situation. Rachel's college appears to have excellent security, and she is street-smart, never going out alone and only going to places that she knows to be safe. I don't think she would give up this experience for anything. But it is still unsettling to me.

The American influence is greatly felt here. Many television programs are in English, and American movies and music are everywhere. We even watch the Miami Dolphins' disastrous play-off game. American philanthropy is evident everywhere too. There's even a plaque on the entrance to the toilet at the Israeli Museum. Alan Greenberg dedicated it to his brother; I think his name was John. Everyone we've met has either been to America or dreams of going there. We feel no antagonism as Americans, which we occasionally did in Greece, although the animosity was more against Bill Clinton than us personally with the Kosovo incident going on at the time.

The weather is quite the departure too. I pictured the desert—you know, warm, sandy, sunny, dry. But we just had eighteen inches of snow dumped on us here in Jerusalem. Unbelievable! At least it slows down the drivers. The ones who dare to go out creep along the road like tired turtles. We have four-wheel drive, so we enjoy a bit of road revenge—until the morning, when our battery dies. Such are the joys of owning a car. A nice gentleman who works at the camera shop recommends a reliable service garage, but in true Israeli fashion, he gives us only sketchy directions and cannot, try as he might, give us an address. We find an address for the garage in the Yellow Pages. This is going to be a challenge. Michael drives most excellently; he can take a left, right, or U-turn upon my command and with little warning. I give orders as if I know what I am doing, in the hopes that by sounding positive, I might just pull it off.

We head out in the general direction of the shop and drive for about ten minutes until it seems like we should be close.

"Take a right here," I say, and Michael hangs a right on a street with no name.

We go two blocks farther, and as we pass another street with no name, I say, "Take a left here."

We drive a few blocks until we come to a garage with a name on it, but in Hebrew. However, the number twenty-four is in English, and much to Michael's amazement (and my own astonishment, although I feign nonchalance), it's the place.

The shop is chock-full of broken-down old heaps. The snowstorm is apparently the final nail in the coffin for a number of ailing vehicles. The owner of the shop is pleasant, but everyone who pulls up just barges right in and begins a conversation with him. It doesn't matter that he is trying to help someone else at that moment. Unfortunately, if you are the only one being polite, it gets you nowhere, so when in Israel, you must be as pushy as the next guy. No problem. In short order, the mechanic fixes up our heap, and we are good to go. Our four-wheel adventures can continue.

We drive south to Eilat. In this resort town, the people are much more laid-back than in Jerusalem. The weather is warm, sunny, and clear—a welcome respite from cold, rainy Jerusalem. The beaches are not as nice as in Florida, but the view across the Red Sea of the mountains of Jordan and Aqaba makes up for it. Spectacular clear blue water hides a coral reef just a few feet off the shore. At this time of year, the tourists are mostly European. There are water activities as far as the eye can see—sailing, snorkeling, scuba diving, windsurfing, and parasailing. The water temperature is barely tolerable, and the air is a bit cool for lengthy swims. We'll come back in a couple of weeks and scuba dive a little farther down into the Sinai in what is now Egypt, where the diving is touted as the best in the world.

The shops and restaurants in the center of town are touristy and tacky. Huge hotels sprawl over the entire northern stretch of beach, and the airport is located smack in the middle of town. The southern beaches are mostly public. A boardwalk running along the shore offers some fun hangouts. We stay in a hotel the first couple of nights and then take a two-day trip to Petra, Jordan.

Jordan

The border crossing to Jordan is about ten minutes from Eilat. We don't take our car across because that would involve an enormous amount of paperwork and money. Walking across is fairly simple, just time-consuming. One Jordanian official scrutinizes our passports as if his life depends on it—come to think of it, his life probably does depend on it. He pastes real stamps on the visa (about ten of them per passport), and then another person checks the computer to make sure we have no history of evildoing and charges us a fee, which varies depending upon which country you come from. Once on the other side, it's a short cab ride to Aqaba, where we pick up a taxi to take us to Petra, a two-hour ride. We luck out with a driver who takes great pride in showing us the scenic route and drives safely. Once out of Aqaba, a beautiful little coastal town opposite Eilat along the Red Sea, the terrain becomes mountainous and empty, save for several Bedouin encampments. The mountains are barren in this part of the country. There's hardly a tree to be seen, but multicolored rock in a variety of textures creates beautiful natural paintings.

As we climb higher into the mountains, there is still snow left from the same storm that hit Jerusalem. Our cab driver, Mohammed, behaves like a kid when he sees it; he obviously doesn't see snow very often. He stops the cab, and we all get out for a stretch and some photos. He plays in the snow with his bare hands and then packs some of it on his windshield to look at while he drives the steep, narrow mountain roads.

We arrive that afternoon in Wadi Moussa, the town closest to Petra, check into a hotel for a one-night stay, and arrange to have Mohammed meet us late the next day for the return trip. We off-load our overnight bags at the hotel and walk down the steep hill to the entrance gate of Petra, not sure what to expect. Petra, known as the rose-red city, is the legacy of the Nabataens, an Arab people who settled in south Jordan more than 2,000 years ago. It is along the route of the camel caravans that carried spices and silks, known as the Spice Route, that led from the coast of Yemen through the desert to the coast of Akko in Israel. Petra is hidden in the rock, virtually invisible until you enter through the gate. Nearly 70,000 people lived in this vast city of caves carved into the sandstone mountains. They buried their dead in tombs carved into the mountains as well. The caves vary from elaborate carvings to more simple dugouts.

Once we enter, the magic begins. First, you walk along a dirt road for a mile past tombs carved into the rocks. Alongside the narrow road is a path for horses, carriages, and donkeys to carry those who choose to travel in this fashion. All roads lead to the Siq, a narrow, mile-long gorge hemmed in by huge cliffs (about 300 feet high). This is the main entrance into Petra.

The first glimpse of El Khazneh (the Treasury) is truly breathtaking. It is a tomb carved into the rock that sits at the end of the Siq, measuring 135 feet from top to bottom and 100 feet wide. The rock, a magnificent rose color, becomes more intense as it catches the late afternoon sun. Its current claim to fame is that *Indiana Jones and the Last Crusade* starring Harrison Ford was filmed here; the famous scene taking place in El Khazneh is touted by all the guides. Everyone, from our cab driver on, seems to have had an opportunity to be best friends with "Harry Ford." The movie is showing at most of the hotels. The power of the media!

Touring Petra is a five-mile walk from one end to the other. Close to the end of the city is a climb of 800 stairs leading up a rock mountain to the Al Deir monastery. Along the way are some of the most colorful, fantastic rock formations imaginable. At the top of the stone stairs, Al Deir (which is "monastery" in Arabic) greets you. Michael and I agree that this is perhaps the most incredible sight we've ever seen. It is a monumental building carved out of the rock mountain, ringed by a view for miles and miles. We take a break from our hike to absorb the scene and hear a flute echoing in the hills. We follow the sound and come upon a Bedouin man standing on a peak, playing his hand-made instrument. He speaks a little English, and we learn that he and his family live on the outskirts of Petra in a small village where many of the service people live. We also find out that his best friend is ... Harrison Ford! He proudly tells us that he was featured in *National Geographic*. A colorful character indeed, he makes a great contribution to our magical experience.

After hours spent walking around Petra, we are hungry and tired, and our legs feel like lead weights as the long uphill climb to our hotel looms before us. Hauling our tired bodies up the hill, we decide to have dinner at our hotel, no matter what they are serving. We have a delicious Arab dish, a combination of rice, tender bits of lamb, vegetables, and exotic seasonings—just spicy enough to be interesting—with grilled flatbread that is chewy and satisfying. This is served with an assortment of salads, including humus, cucumber in yogurt and dill, and assorted olives. The next day is sunny and cool, so we get off to an early start. We walk around for hours, just absorbing as much as possible.

On our way back, I can't resist any longer. I simply have to try riding a camel—a dromedary, to be exact. (There are two types of camels—a dromedary has one hump, and a Bactrian has two.) Now that's a different ride. You sit high up, wrap one leg around the hump, and kind of roll in sync with the camel's gait. I am led around in a circle; it is a surprisingly smooth ride. I'd be game for a half-day trek in the desert, but that's not going to happen. Michael has done this before; he dislikes camels and hates riding them.

Mohammed the cab driver comes as planned to take us back to the Eilat border. About halfway back, we make a stop at Wadi Rum to watch the sunset and drink tea in a Bedouin tent. We are mesmerized as the setting sun catches the tops of the mountains. This environment, so different from anything we have experienced to date, evokes intense feelings. My very soul is awakened in a way that I have never felt before. If only I could bottle up this combination of feelings—peace, wonderment, awe, life, reincarnation—and pull it out again when needed.

Back to Israel

We cross the Jordanian border back into Israel that evening, and in a few minutes we are back at our hotel in Eilat.

The following day, we check out of the hotel and make our way to a campsite across from Coral Beach. It feels so good to gaze out over the Red Sea and do our outdoorsy camping thing. It never rains here, so camping is a trusty alternative. It's certainly preferable to paying for hotels with mediocre beds, unexciting breakfast, and noisy neighbors. We set up the canopy tent that Holk gave us, which serves as an extension to the Subaru and gives us a living room under cover, warm and private. We set up our sleeping tent beneath the extension. We may have been too thrifty on the purchase of the sleeping bags, however. I fit into mine well enough, but getting Michael tucked into his proves quite an ordeal. We've got it down to a science now: Michael scoots down into the bag, I zip. More scooting down and a little more zipping, until at last he's all in. Michael is swaddled like a mummy and stays toasty warm, since there is no room for any cold air. Rolling over is out of the question. Still, he claims that he's sleeping better than ever.

The evenings are cool, maybe in the fifties, but the days warm up enough for T-shirts and shorts. We cook our own breakfasts, usually pack up a lunch to take on our outings, and eat dinner out. Only two other couples are camping here; we enjoy conversing with them. We camp for a week and could have stayed on for a month with no problem, but we're paying rent for our apartment in Jerusalem, and it seems a shame not to use it.

On the way back to Jerusalem, we drive to Maktesh Ramon, a humungous crater in the middle of the Negev desert. We decide to camp at the National Park in the middle of the crater for the evening. We are the only campers. The Bedouin who operate the large tent and campsite are preparing to serve dinner to a busload of 150 students arriving for the traditional Bedouin dinner and stories. We are invited to join them for dinner. Afterward, the tour group moves on. We stay by the fire in the Bedouin tent, drinking tea and smoking a dried apple mixture from a water pipe, which the Bedouin call a *nargila*.

One of the young Bedouin speaks English, so he entertains us with stories about his family and the customs of Bedouin life. He looks like a young Omar Sharif—dark skin, straight white teeth, brown eyes, and absolutely gorgeous. He has twenty-three brothers and sisters—his father has two wives, although they are allowed up to four. He enjoys practicing his English, and we listen with rapt attention. The term *Bedu* in the Arabic language refers to one who lives out in the open, in the desert. The Arabic word *Badawiyin* is a generic name for a desert-dweller; the English word Bedouin is derived from this. The Bedouin are recognized by their nomadic lifestyles, language, social structures, and culture. Only a few Bedouin live as their forefathers did. Their numbers are decreasing. Nowadays, in all the Middle East, only five percent of Bedouin still live as pastoral nomads.

We hike around a part of the crater and climb up a rocky mountain at the north end, thrilled by the panoramic view. The pattern of the crater's erosion allows geologists to identify fossils and ancient rock formations dating back 220 million years. Some of the formations consist of beautiful multicolored sandstone.

The Negev desert is fascinating. The word desert conjures up "hot, dry, and barren." Actually, the Negev highlands are cold in the winter, particularly at night, and extremely hot in the summer, but dry all year round. There is a surprising variety of plant life and animals, but people have to be observant to find them at this time of year. We are told that in spring the lowlands of the crater and the lower lands of the desert in general are blanketed with wildflowers. Manmade irrigation makes it possible to grow trees, plants, vegetables, and other crops. Many *kibbutzim* are located in the fertile Negev.

On our way back to Jerusalem, we go through Be'er Sheva, where a population of 65,000 Bedouin lives. The Bedouin set up their camps using tarpaper, stones, corrugated metal for roofs and walls, gutted-out vehicles, old doors and shutters, and whatever else they can find. It is bizarre. Goats, donkeys, sheep, and the occasional camel wander in and around these structures. I have no idea what the livestock grazes on—there doesn't seem to be a blade of grass in sight. The camps are in wide-open desert hills with no trees or bushes to provide any kind of shelter. They are generally unappealing—not at all like the nomad dwellings in Turkey, which were in woody, hilly settings. But I still love the concept of Bedouin life, and Michael and I are proud to be considered by some to be full-fledged Bedouin. We definitely meet the criteria. We have no permanent home, we prefer living outdoors, and we love our sheep, goats, and camels—well, two out of three.

* * *

I can't believe a year has gone by since we sold our house in Coral Gables and became homeless. I'm trying to remember what it was like back then. Oh, yeah—rising at dawn; fighting traffic to get to work; sweating like crazy in business suits; juggling my beeper, cell phone, and cup of coffee in the car; stressing over deals and money that was due me; and trying to make time for a workout, food shopping, preparing meals, errands, more errands, and more errands. And life was not bad at all. In fact, it was good. But this ... this past year has been incredible, and our adventure continues. We'll make certain of that. I am not ready to go back and don't know when I will be.

Al Deir Monastery

Harrison Ford's best friend

The Treasury

CHAPTER 16

Up, Down, and
Around Israel

I have found out that there ain't no surer way to find
out whether you like people or hate them than to travel
with them.

—Mark Twain

Now that Michael and I have been traveling for over a year, I have
made a rather horrifying observation: we're starting to look like each
other. The clothes we originally brought with us from the States have
been washed and worn to death and are steadily being replaced. For
example, hiking boots—we found a pair we both liked and both bought
them. Gray and white T-shirts were reasonably priced, and we both
bought them. Blue unisex safari pants? Both gotta have 'em. Baseball
caps are a must in the burning sun for both heads. Without planning our
wardrobes, we get dressed in the morning and end up wearing exactly
the same thing from head to foot. Michael even bought underpants
that, in a pinch, I can borrow, especially since they turned pink at the
Laundromat. Separating colors is a thing of the past. Well, the good
news is the weather is finally warming up, so I'll be the one wearing a
tank top and maybe the pink undies.

Other than the jogs and walks that I take by myself, we are in each
other's company twenty-four hours a day. This is truly a test of our
relationship. We are sharing the experiences of traveling and living in
new places. Gradually we are learning to relax and go with the flow—
not let the minutiae bother us. We have this unique opportunity to

wake up and breathe in the beauty of the day and the wonderment of what is to come. During this time, we are getting to know each other on a deeper level. We are not watching TV. We don't socialize with others very often, due to the language differences. We are not preoccupied with children, homes, and jobs, as we were in the past. So, we talk with each other. We discuss the books we are reading, the differences in cultures, and where our next destination will be. But mostly we talk about how fortunate we are, and we share this almost secret glee in what we are doing.

We must go to the customs office in Haifa in order to extend the registration on our automobile. Ready for our little adventure, we hop in our Subaru and head west toward Tel Aviv and then north until we arrive in Haifa two hours later. We go to the port, get customs all squared away, and continue north to visit the ancient walled city of Akko. We spend the afternoon and early evening walking around this historic seaport and have a wonderful dinner at a waterfront restaurant: grilled trout with a bottle of good red wine from the local vineyard.

Well-fed and pleased with ourselves for having accomplished the mission, we head back to Jerusalem the way we came. Traffic toward Haifa is terrible. Nothing is moving, and we know it will only get worse as we approach Tel Aviv. I have my flashlight and map on my lap, looking for an alternative route. No problem. I see a way back that should avoid all the traffic. It appears to be fairly direct, bringing us back to Jerusalem from the north. All righty, then—we decide to go for it. We are good for a while until the road brings us straight into Nazareth, with no clue as to how to get out again. Now it is about ten o'clock on a pitch-black night, but we manage to wind up and down the hills, with hairpin turns that literally make the hair on our necks stick up like pins.

Finally, we see a sign for our desired highway. The road quickly turns into a pitted, curvy one-lane muddle, with no evidence of civilization and occasional unmarked forks in the road. We just wing it for about two hours, running low on gas and high on anxiety, until we finally find an open gas station. The attendant, in full Palestinian garb, tries to give us directions, but we end up just nodding to be polite. The bathroom here is the worst I've ever seen, and I've seen a few shitholes in our travels. Michael stands guard while I use it, leaving the door open—there is no light, and it stinks, and oh jeez, those dreaded treadmills. When I finish, Michael takes his turn—he stands at the threshold and aims into the darkness. I later learn that we made this pit stop in Jenin, the headquarters of Hamas.

We continue on until we come to a barricade. At the checkpoint, we are waved to pull over. Uh-oh. These are not Israeli soldiers; these are Palestinian soldiers. The keffiyeh (black-and-white checked headscarf), along with the uniforms and Uzis, are a dead giveaway. They come over to my side of the window, and I show them my handy flashlight and map, innocently asking them if this is the way to Jerusalem. Another soldier comes over, missing teeth and all, and they smile and ask us where we are from. They speak a couple of words in English, which we interpret (perhaps wishfully) to be, "Yes, this is the right road. It is safe—no problem."

We think our Swiss license plates are helpful in establishing the fact that we are nonthreatening tourists. We are absolutely smack in the middle of the West Bank—Palestinian Autonomous Territory. But we have to continue on. I, for one, do not want to go back through that checkpoint.

We drive through small, extremely poor Arab villages that are completely dark and look almost uninhabited. The roads are pitted and have unexpected speed bumps that must have been created to stop a tank and nearly wipe us out. Michael stays focused on driving, his expression intense. He has been driving for hours by now. We are both on the edge of our seats, peering into the pitch black to see if the road continues, terrified that it will be a dead end and we will be screwed. Another hour of this, and we get to yet another checkpoint. We've had time to plan for this one, and we tell them we are trying to get to Ramallah (an Arab city, the home of Yasser Arafat, just a few miles north of Jerusalem). They nod and smile and indicate to us that we are headed the right way. By this time, I tell Michael, "I'll be so glad to see signs in Hebrew!"

We figure the road conditions can't get much worse. No sooner do we say that than the fog settles in.

At last, we begin seeing familiar names. We made it, four and a half hours after we started. Well, we did avoid all traffic, and it was the right direction. And now we can say it was truly an enlightening experience. We feel comfortable in the neighborhoods of Jerusalem or Eilat or Tel Aviv, but just a few miles away, it's a different world—a country within a country. You can't appreciate the physical relationship until you see it. The Arabs have treated Michael and me well enough, but the underlying tension is there, very close by.

Once recovered, we take a trip north through the Jordan Valley to Galilee and the Golan Heights. The landscape is green and lush, soothing for the body and soul. We camp out at the water's edge of Lake Kinneret (also known as the Sea of Galilee), looking toward Tiberius, set along the hillside on the opposite side of the lake. The campsite is not officially open this time of year, so we have the entire place to ourselves. Over the next few days, we cover the area quite thoroughly. We walk through the Hula Reserve with its "everglades," its tropical flora and fauna. We hike up and around Nimrod's Castle, drive up Mt. Hermon to the ski resort, hike through Banyas Nature Reserve, go to Tel Dan, visit Kiryat Shimona, and get up close and personal with the border of Lebanon (about two miles up the road) before heading back down to Tiberius.

The weather varies wildly. It is sunny and warm by the lake and snowing at the top of Mt. Hermon. It never ceases to amaze me that for such a tiny country, it has everything from year-round beach resorts to skiing, lush green valleys to desert canyons. It makes for a fascinating variety of activities and a terrific adventure.

Now that the weather has warmed up, we've been to the Dead Sea a few times and we're totally into the activity of covering ourselves with the therapeutic mineral mud, soaking in the hot springs, and bobbing along as though weightless in the salty Dead Sea. Rachel and her friends come with us on one of our outings, and we have some good laughs taking pictures of ourselves doing a classic "Creatures of the Mud" routine. Michael is fascinated by the fact that there are lifeguards along the water's edge.

He says to one guard, "This has to be the most boring job in Israel. There is no way one can drown in this water."

"On the contrary," says the lifeguard. "When the fat tourists are showing off by floating on their backs, nonchalantly reading a magazine for the photo op, they invariably flip over on their stomachs. Like helpless turtles, they have to be flipped face up again. Happens all the time."

One morning we hike up the Mount of Olives, dominated by the world's oldest and largest Jewish cemetery. Among the tombs we are greeted by Jacob, a sweet elderly Arab—also a self-appointed gravesite tour guide. He insists on bringing us to Schindler's grave. We take pictures of him and the gravesite, bid him farewell with hugs and shekels, and finally manage to disengage ourselves. After I get the pictures developed, Rachel impresses us with her knowledge of Hebrew and reads the script on Schindler's grave. It says Rosie Schwartz!

* * *

We have to move out of our apartment in the French Hill district after two and half months since it had been booked prior to our arrival, and we relocate to a different neighborhood. This turns out to be a great move. Ramot is quite upscale, perched on a hill surrounded by a forest below. Spring is here, we have our new hiking boots, and now we are renting a house close to abundant woods. Our spirits are high. The day after we move in, neighbors in the adjacent house invite Michael, Rachel, and me to join her family for Shabbat dinner. She also invites Rosine, our landlady, and her teenage son. Rachele and Menachem are wonderful hosts. We do a traditional Shabbat, in an atmosphere of warmth and sharing—all the good things that Shabbat represents.

Rachele and Menachem came to Israel from the United States about seven years ago. Their mission was to give their children "all the things that money can't buy." Michael and I have a better understanding of and new respect for Shabbat since we've lived here. It is a national holiday. On Fridays, everyone is hustling and bustling like crazy to get all their food shopping and errands done before sundown, when the air-raid siren blows to notify you that Shabbat has begun. I find it ironic that the Muslims' *muezzin* sing over the loud speakers to notify their people of prayer times, the Christians ring church bells, and the Israelis blast the air-raid sirens. *Hmmm.* Whether or not the Sabbath is strictly observed, it is a time for people to be with their families. Preparations for meals and such are made in advance so that all energies can be focused on reading, contemplation, and a timeout from the hectic, fast-paced way of life here.

Meanwhile, the development of Israel has created difficulties for some of the Bedouin tribes. Although the courts have ruled that the Civil Administration must provide alternative sites before moving them from their traditional lands, in some cases it required them to move to a spot where it would be impossible to maintain their traditional lifestyle. While some of the younger Bedouin are looking forward to moving out of tents and into the permanent houses being provided for them, many of the tribes sense that moving into even the most luxurious of houses would be a tragedy, a painful end to their traditional way of life. Programs are being established to help the Bedouin assimilate into the Israeli society. An organization called Rabbis for Human Rights has developed activities to strengthen the connection with the Bedouin families. They are working with volunteers from Hebrew University to tutor the children in English and young adults in Hebrew. Recently, they've added instruction in computer skills.

Rachel and I join a group from Hebrew University that has been working with a particular Bedouin tribe on the outskirts of Jerusalem. The condition of the temporary encampment is deplorable. There is no plumbing, no electric hookups, and no place on this particular dirt pile for animals to graze. The children are wide-eyed, smiling, and beautiful, golden-skinned with rosy cheeks and greenish-brown eyes. They are delighted to have us visit them for a couple of hours, and the parents are appreciative as well. We come prepared with pencils and paper, crayons, and, to the delight of the little children, Disney stickers. The program is a bit unstructured, and I'm not sure if the kids learn many new words. Hopefully, though, they feel the love and caring we desperately want to give them and a sense that there is hope.

Michael and I get to play tour guide for our travel soul mates, Dana and Warren Cohn, who come to stay with us for two weeks. Our itinerary is full and varied, and their timing is perfect—April in Israel is spectacular. During the course of the two weeks, we cover Israel from the Sea of Galilee to the Dead Sea and the Red Sea. The town of Safed particularly intrigues us. It's also spelled Tzfad, Zefad, or Tsfat—typical of Israel, where everything is spelled at least three different ways. It is a gorgeous hilltop town with a rich heritage. The people of the town draw you in, eager to share the "mysticism, miracles, and art" that Safed is known for.

We enjoy talking with the residents. One lovely elderly couple invites us to their home for a glass of wine. They tell us quite a few stories about immigrating to Israel from Germany after the Second World War and fighting in the 1948 War of Independence for the State of Israel. When settling into their home in Safed over fifty years ago, they planted seeds for a fig tree. As we were saying good-bye, this sweet lady said, "My dream is to have all the Jewish people in the world come to Safed and sit in peace under the leaves of our beautiful, now fully-grown fig tree."

Another young woman we encounter moved from Manhattan a year ago with her husband and two babies. She found Safed to be a safe and affordable place to raise her children. She tells us there are seventy-five *shuls* (Hebrew religious schools). During the evening the entire population is chanting and preparing to enjoy the Shabbat dinner. Many of the artists are world-renowned; they seem to enjoy chatting with us about their work and their lives. Michael, Dana, Warren, and I are deeply enchanted with Safed. Sharing this time with our friends is a perfect way to end our Israeli adventure.

Dana and Warren's e-mail to us on their return to the states says it beautifully:

> Hi to BTG [Bedouin Tour Guides], Ramot 2, the Bedouin mobile, the Old City, poached trout with almonds, kippas of every size and design, chanting black beards and robes at night at the Western Wall, Abed singing "Dana, Dana, Dana," the Sea of Galilee shower, soothing mineral baths, floating in the Dead Sea, coral reefs, parrot fish, eggs every day and every way, warm conversations, laughter, hugs, friendship, our children, chocolate, the scent of orange blossoms, Aviva, the blue warmth of Safed, ancient synagogues, flirting with the sun setting over the changing Jordan landscape, sipping sage tea, chocolate, warm sesame pita, the night sky, the complexities and contrasts of the Israeli people and the Israeli landscape, young Jewish soldiers with weapons, an unexpected Orthodox wedding, Shabbat dinner, chocolate, humus, camels, lunch at Dubrovin Farm, Yehuda market madness, the music and light of Chihuly, Jewish mysticism, spirituality, "attitude" … and so, so much more yet to absorb and to remember, but most importantly, to our special travel guides, friends who made this journey so much more than just a vacation: a reawakening of all our senses, our history, our connection to each other and the cycles of life. We feel blessed … thank you, thank you, thank you, all our love.

Michael and I notice that since we don't have a permanent home and no current jobs, people we meet have a difficult time figuring out which peg to hang us on. They are forced to accept (or reject) us based on what they care to see. I can tell them that we are not only

International Dog Sitters (IDG), but also official Bedouin Tour Guides (BTG), so that ought to clear things up.

But my sense of identity has changed as well. I am not thinking of myself as a businesswoman and mother. I am a traveler—more relaxed and less worried about details, about propriety. I am beginning to see myself and the world from a broader perspective.

* * *

We're packin' 'em up and movin' 'em out again. We'll start out with a few days of sun, surf, and seafood in Dahab, Egypt, with Rachel, her stateside friend Meredith, and another friend Alex, who's visiting from London. Then we will take a ferryboat out from Haifa and stop briefly in Cyprus before we arrive in Rhodes, Greece. And, at last, we will return to further explore Turkey.

Shalom, Israel.

Rachel and I with Bedouin children

Taxi stand, Eilat

CHAPTER 17

Return to Turkey

Happiness is when what you think, what you say, and what you do are in harmony.

—Mahatma Gandhi

Leaving Haifa, we take a Cypriot ferryboat to Rhodes. The three-day trip on calm seas is pleasantly different from our *Poseidon* adventure a few months ago. In Rhodes, we make arrangements for a car ferry to take us on the two-hour ride over to Marmaris, on the southern coast of Turkey. It's no easy feat—two days later, the arrangements are completed. We pay a rather exorbitant amount for this, but have no choice in the matter—only one agent arranges ferryboats for passengers with vehicles to Marmaris. Three cars are lined up to go aboard: a huge Mercedes, probably worth about US$75,000; a twenty-foot Peugeot station wagon worth about US$40,000; and our twelve-foot-long Subaru, worth US$4,500. Michael is peeved because we paid twice as much as they did; we made the mistake of calling it a "minibus," an unfortunate description that set off bells and whistles and comments like, "Congratulations—you get to pay double."

The ferry is the size of a small tugboat. Michael drives the car up a narrow ramp onto the deck of the boat while I take pictures, just in case, although I'm pretty sure our insurance company doesn't cover overboard disasters. They place a wooden block behind the wheel, and a handful of passengers go inside. The Mercedes belongs to an absolutely delightful Englishman named Roger Arscott. We quickly become friends. Roger manages a four-star hotel called L'Etoile in Içmeler, the town right next to Marmaris, where we started our sailing trip on the *Pitawama* last June, almost one year ago. Since we have no reservations for a hotel thus far, we decide to stay there. Sometimes no plans are the best plans. The ferry trip ends up being delightful, and all vehicles disembark safely.

Going through customs is uneventful, and we drive a short way to L'Etoile. Roger makes us feel like dignitaries, and the off-season price with half-board—meaning that breakfast and dinner are included—is only US$25 a day for both of us. We settle into this comfortable hotel and enjoy the company of Roger and his wife, Anne, several times for dinner and drinks. Içmeler is a charming little coastal town. Our window faces the bay, which is dotted with small islands blanketed with wildflowers and trees. The supermarket (Migros, a Swiss company) is as clean and spiffy as any we've seen in our travels, and everything is inexpensive. There are several cafés and restaurants (everything from Chinese to Korean, Mexican, and Turkish, sometimes in the same restaurant), and the food is good. There is a walkway around the coastline from Içmeler to Marmaris, which takes about an hour and a half. Resorts line the way, as do cafés and bars in which to sit and sip tea or drink *raki*. They call this stretch of coastline the Turkish Riviera. The people are friendly, and we are relishing our time here. The tourists are mostly English and German with a scattering of Israelis, but few Americans.

Picture this: a clear, breezy day, midseventies, fields of red poppies and yellow flowers, and grass that is lush green after the previous rainy season. Mountains provide the backdrop for the village; roosters and chickens peck nearby. Michael and I are on our newly purchased, slightly used bicycles, cruising at slow speed around the old village of Içmeler. Our basket is filled with tuna sandwiches, fruit, and cheese. We find the perfect picnic spot, park the bikes, spread out a towel, and lay out the goodies when we notice a young Turkish man heading directly toward us. He hands us two ice-cold bottles of Coca-Cola and says, "From me to you. Please enjoy," and then he heads back to his little market about fifty meters away.

This is Turkey.

We got a taste of this area a year ago when we landed in Marmaris for our sailing trip, and now we have the time to further explore. This huge country is terribly poor, with an average annual income of about US$6,500. The dollar is strong right now—about 618,000 Turkish liras to the dollar—so it is inexpensive for Michael and me to live here. Dinner for two at a moderate restaurant costs us about US$16 (nearly 10 million lira). We just came back from the supermarket and bought a head of lettuce, three tomatoes, two zucchini, three large onions, four bananas, three cucumbers, and a small bag of potatoes, all for the equivalent of US$2.25. A loaf of fresh-baked bread is twelve cents. Membership in a fitness center in a five-star hotel is offered for ten visits, including classes and full use of the equipment, for a grand total of US$20. The price is right! Gasoline is expensive, about the same as in Europe, but we can bicycle or take ferries or buses just about everywhere. Car rentals are expensive, but we have our trusty Subaru minibus. About the only thing we can't do here is work, as permits are difficult to obtain. But who's thinking about working?

The Turks with whom we've spoken are so curious about America. We are a novelty here. They would love to travel, but obtaining a visa is difficult for them and cost-prohibitive. They have learned to speak English and German from the tourists. The young people watch MTV, just like everywhere else in the world. Last year, we were impressed with the hospitality of the people here and their desire to show their country in its best light, and we have not been disappointed on this return visit.

Our friend Roger brings us to a charming corner restaurant near the hotel in Içmeler, owned and run by Suleyman ("Charlie Sheen" is his American name—everyone has a moniker to share with the tourists). He's a young, bright, handsome Turk whose company we enjoy. The season doesn't kick in until the middle of May, so we are his only customers for about a week. He tells us about a small apartment building next door to his restaurant. We decide to check it out, and with Suleyman's help in the negotiations with the owner, we make a deal. We are now settled in a small, one-bedroom apartment for the month of May and pay about US$10 a day—furnished, with daily maid service. Of course, Suleyman's kitchen functions like an extension of our place. We just pop over and ask, "What's for dinner?" and have a tasty, authentic Turkish meal.

Turkish food is satisfying and healthy: fresh fish, which is plentiful in the waters here, grilled meats (lamb, chicken, or beef), and numerous vegetable dishes. One of my favorites so far is called *güveç*. It's a casserole of zucchini, potatoes, mushrooms, and eggplant cooked in a tomato base, sometimes served with melted cheese on top. Our favorite restaurant for this dish is a little place, well off the beaten path in Içmeler and owned by a local family. The Turkish waiter is friendly, speaks a little English, and takes our order. Midway through the meal, our waiter has changed clothes and now is in full drag queen regalia. The music changes to disco, and he begins dancing. His makeup is running a little, but he is dancing with no inhibitions. When the song is finished, he comes to our table to see if we need anything. Michael declines his kiss—and I order a strong drink!

The tomatoes and strawberries right now are scrumptious. There are about ten varieties of local honey. Our landlady, Nimet, gives us a traditional Turkish dessert called *aşure*, a treat with a pudding-like consistency made of figs, small white beans, walnuts, chestnuts, apricots, raisins, and a barley-like grain, flavored with nutmeg and cinnamon and topped with peanuts. I am listing the ingredients to the best of my knowledge, not having found a Turkish cookbook in English yet and having limited ability to understand Nimet, who speaks English about as well as I speak Turkish—lots of hand movements and body language. This creamy confection is different from anything we've tasted. We devour it. We are told that at this time of the year it is customary to make a batch of *aşure* and give it to friends and neighbors. *Afiyet olsun* (bon appétit).

The last week of May, we fly to Istanbul and stay for five nights and six days. This city of about 13 million people is full of life and engages all the senses. It is beautiful, with various seas and rivers surrounding and running through it. It is user-friendly; its public transportation is excellent, not to mention fun. Trams and ferries cost practically nothing, and I've never seen so many *taksis* in my life. Each neighborhood of Istanbul has its own ambience. The food is extraordinary and reasonable. Our hotel, called the Nomade Otel, is perfectly located in the heart of the Sultanahmet area. We have a view of the famous Blue Mosque and are right above a charming little alley with cafés, bars, and of course, carpet stores galore. There are gorgeous parks to meander through, and we are near all the important sites and museums. It's the perfect place for first-time visitors.

There are eighty-five mosques in the city and one on the block next to ours, so we are reminded five times a day that we are in an Islamic country. First call from the *muezzin* is at five in the morning, and the next call to prayer follows at eight. In the early morning quiet, we can hear the *muezzin* from the other mosques throughout the area—almost like an echo, or "dueling *muezzin*," as Michael and I refer to them. I love it. I can actually do a fairly good rendition—Michael says I sound as though I'm in serious pain, possibly overdosed on *donar kebabs*.

It doesn't take too long to get street-smart about the carpet salesmen. They wander throughout the area (particularly in Sultanahmet) looking for the slightly confused, awestruck tourists and offer friendly advice, such as when the Blue Mosque is open, where the Hagia Sofia is, and by the way, "My carpet shop is right this way—no obligation, just come in and have some tea." Well, okay, since you put it that way. We are lucky, however. Our carpet salesman/tour guide/tea server is pleasant and knowledgeable. Before giving him the bad news that we have no house and therefore do not need a carpet, we get a good education on Turkish rugs—how they are made, types of materials, meanings of the patterns, range of prices, etc. He lays down about fifteen rugs. The last sales pitch was, "If you could buy one of these for US$100, which one would you like?" When we say none, his demeanor changes radically. He is through with us and shows us to the door before we can thank him for our newfound knowledge. Next!

* * *

Istanbul attracts interesting people like Sarah and Tom. They are about our age, live in Vermont, and have been traveling for about five months prior to their Turkey visit. They've been to Thailand, Bali, New Zealand, Australia, and most recently India. Tom is still recuperating from India and eats conservatively when we go out for meals together. They are carrying some pretty serious backpacks. I am silently sending happy kudos to our Subaru. There is no way that I could carry a heavy backpack and still enjoy the trip! We may hook up with Tom and Sarah in a month or so, since our paths will be crossing somewhere on the Mediterranean coast. By sharing ideas with fellow travelers, we learn about other places that could be of interest to us. The beauty of not having an agenda is that it gives us the freedom to go where and when we please. We are developing the skill of simply loafing, taking our time, and taking the easiest path. Flexible schedules, flexible spirits.

We are also taken with a British woman who has been living with her husband and two children in Saudi Arabia for the past twenty-two years. I meet another woman on the ferry that we take up the Bosphorus. She is a grandmother, well on in years, and has been traveling for the past twelve of them. She goes back to her home in Vancouver, Canada, every three months or so just to regroup, take care of business, have her health checkups, and so on, and then she's off again. I love her youthful spirit.

Our *Go Turkey* guidebook has once again proven invaluable. We hit all the must-sees, plus a few that were not on the list, including the mystical underground cistern. As we descend into this dark and cool cavern beneath the city's center, we are greeted by the somber strains of Bach. An overturned head of Medusa lies in the eerily lit shallow waters beneath the metal walkway, an otherworldly effect not to be missed. The entrance to the Basilica Cistern of Istanbul is across the street from the Hagia Sophia, in Sultanahmet. This immense underground water container was built during the reign of Emperor Justinian I in AD 532 to meet the water needs of the Great Palace. This marvelous piece of engineering only confirms, yet again, that this was the heyday of the Byzantine Empire. The Basilica Cistern could hold 80,000 cubic meters of water and comes from the *Eğrikapı* Water Distribution Centre in the Belgrade Forest, nineteen kilometers from the city. The water was transported to the city center via the 971-meter-long Valens Aqueduct (*Bozdoğan Sukemeri*) and the 11,545-meter-long *Mağlova* Aqueduct, which was built by Emperor Justinian I. The cistern was forgotten for centuries and only accidently rediscovered by the Frenchman Peter Gyllius in 1545. While researching Byzantine antiquities in the city, he noticed that people in the neighborhood not only got ahold of water by simply lowering buckets through holes in their basements, they miraculously sometimes even caught fish this way.

Another highlight of our trip is the ninety-minute ferry ride north up the Bosphorus Straits to the entrance of the Black Sea, where the ferry stops for a couple of hours. We walk up a steep road to an old fort and enjoy the view from the top of the cliff looking out onto the Black Sea to the north and down along the Bosphorus Straits to the west. Lunch is at a waterside café: freshly caught fish, grilled, with a salad. We take the ferry back and relish the golden late-afternoon sunlight that shines on the European side of the Bosphorus Straits, highlighting its magnificent palatial structures.

We have a funny experience in a restaurant while lunching with Tom and Sarah. We are showing pictures of our kids to them as the waiter peers over our shoulders. He gets terribly excited about a picture of Michael with a beard, claiming that he looks just like a famous Turkish actor. He asks if he can borrow the picture to show the owner of the restaurant. Before we know it, there are four Turkish men looking at the picture, then Michael, then the picture, and so on. He returns and insists on putting a fez on Michael's head. And then a sultan's robe. By this time we are all rolling with laughter, except for the waiter. He is in love. He cannot take his eyes off Michael for the entire lunch. I ask for a cup of tea and am totally ignored. Michael is a great sport about it and only a bit concerned when the waiter tags along when he excuses himself to use the men's room.

It is the perfect stay, and we cover a lot of territory in those few days. We are ready to go back to our southern coastal paradise for a little rest from our vacation.

* * *

Our paradise has been invaded by "Hey Mambo, Mambo Italiano." I don't know why the Turks think loud music will attract business. Maybe they need it to stay pumped up and smiling twenty-four hours a day and to be able to ask every passing tourist, "Hello, excuse me, where are you from?"

All the outdoor cafés, restaurants, and bars have huge speakers blasting music. Even at our little apartment building, which has a pool with an outdoor bar, there is a young bartender named Eric (his Americanized name, of course) who plays music nonstop. Each morning he wakes us up with his favorite, "Mambo Italiano," and during the day he repeats it at least twenty-five times. The other favorite of his has a Latin beat with the only lyrics being, "If you want it, come and get it." Desperate for something a little different, we hand Eric some of the CDs we've been traveling with. We don't realize that we included Celine Dion in the bunch, and wouldn't you know it—Eric loves this CD. Celine Dion is fine to listen to once or twice, but the hundredth time you hear the diva at full blast, it brings on an epileptic fit. I plead with Eric not to play it anymore, even though we gave it to him.

He says, "No, no, I love this song. It is so-o-o-o beautiful!"

Well, it's his bar. And besides, he is so nice and friendly that we haven't the heart to take it back. So we're moving out.

Our friend Roger is letting us stash some of our belongings with him, so we pack up our Subaru with camping stuff, shorts, and bathing suits, and away we go in true nomad style. It's the end of May, and the weather is perfect—warm in the sun, cool in the shade, no humidity. We leave Içmeler and head east along the Mediterranean coast, working our way from one little village to another, with side trips from there. We're eager to explore more of this fascinating country.

Overloaded ferry, Rhodes to Marmaris

Tom and Sarah, Istanbul

Waiter on the right really likes Michael

CHAPTER 18

Travels in Turkey

There are no foreign lands. It is the traveler only who
is foreign.

—Robert Louis Stevenson

At this moment I am sitting at a table that is set up for breakfast
under a peach tree in the garden of the Flower Pension in a tiny village
along the Mediterranean Sea called Patara. There are several chickens
pecking the ground dangerously close to my bare feet. White towels and
sheets hang on the line in the sunny part of the yard, flapping in the easy
morning breeze, and roosters continuously crow—and why not? Life is
so perfect in Patara that I just might join in on a cock-a-doodle-doo or
two. This village is a great combination of traditional Turkish life, with
just enough of a smattering of tourism to make it comfortable for us. If
we walk about twenty minutes down the road, past imposing ruins set
back in dunes that date from about 4,000 years ago, we end up at the
sea on a thirteen-mile stretch of fine sand beach. The sun bakes you
like the traditional Turkish *gözleme* bread, but under the shade of the
umbrella, the temperature is comfortable, and the ocean water is clear,
cool, and refreshing.

For two weeks, we've been traveling Turkey's Mediterranean shore,
called the Turquoise Coast, heading southeast from Içmeler toward
Antalya and beyond. We continue to be captivated by the sheer beauty of
the country and its people. We spent a few days in Koyçegiz, a lakeside
village located in a nature reserve. Highlights of that visit included our
pension, the Flora Motel, and our hosts, Hakan and Alp; waking up
to the sound of the chickens under our bedroom window and the cow
mooing next door; dining alfresco on the motel's porch, which faces

the lake amidst a profusion of flowering trees and bougainvillea; eating homemade Turkish cooking; the hike to the waterfall and watching Alp appear, much to our amazement, just to make sure we didn't get lost; zillions of species of birds in exotic amber trees; the huge weekly bazaar at which (in addition to the usual veggies, olives, and cheese) I was thrilled to find lace undies for eighty cents a pair and fresh loaves of bread wrapped in newspaper (the only recycling we've seen so far); a boat ride to Dalyan, with lunch on board shared with Hakan and his uncle (our captain) consisting of peeled cucumbers, whole juicy sweet tomatoes, hunks of mild white goat cheese, olives, and fresh loaves of bread; and Turtle Island, with a magnificent sand beach on one side and the lake on the other.

✳ ✳ ✳

We continue our travels along the coast and in Dalyan meet up with Tom and Sarah, the American couple we first met in Istanbul. Tom and Sarah are now about six months into their travels and planning on going for another year before returning to their home in Vermont. They seem wonderfully compatible with each other, and we realize that there is absolutely no way a couple can travel together in the fashion that we do without having a special relationship. We exchange notes about places we've been since we started out in opposite directions. The Dalyan campground provides us with comfortable little bungalows on the edge of town right on the shore of the Dalyan River, directly opposite the famous carved Lycian rock tombs. These are the same tombs we visited one year earlier, during our sailing excursion. We have the place to ourselves, and we spend hours sitting on the dock.

The four of us have a beautiful dinner at a French restaurant set under a rubber tree on the banks of the river and enjoy the sun's warm afterglow playing off the tombs carved into the hills. The starters are a nice combination of salads (*mezze*). For dinner, Sarah and I have fresh grilled sea bass with lemon; Michael and Tom have grilled lamb chops. We are brought a finger bowl of rosewater with bougainvillea petals floating on top. Tom can't leave until we have baklava (no arguments from the rest of us) and fresh fruit, which is commonly served after the meal. "A splurge for twenty dollars for two with a bottle of wine," Tom says.

The typical Turkish breakfast, which comes with lodging, is a colorful array of tomatoes, cucumbers, olives, a loaf of bread (*ekmek* in Turkish), jam, honey, a slice of white cheese (feta), a hardboiled egg, and Turkish tea.

After spending four days with Tom and Sarah in Dalyan, Michael and I continued on our own to another gorgeous coastal village called Ölüdeniz, known as the Blue Lagoon. We have never seen water so clear and blue; the white pebble beach only accentuates the color. We stay in a campsite a short walk from the beach called Oba ("nomad" in Turkish—how appropriate). We rent a two-story bungalow with a bathroom for a total of six million lira a night (about US$10, including breakfast). There are cushioned seating areas in various places around the campgrounds and an outdoor restaurant. The only problem is that around ten o'clock at night, the nearby bars start blasting the one and only CD disco mix in Turkey and keep it up until three o'clock in the morning. We stay there for three nights and then can't hack it anymore.

This brings me to the garden in Patara where I am sitting among the chickens and writing on my laptop. Our hosts from the Flower Pension arrange a day trip for us to the Saklikent Gorge. Our American guide calls himself Indiana Jones and he decides we need a bit of a thrill in our lives. We spend ninety minutes walking deep into the gorge on slippery rocks in *cold* rushing water that at times is chest high. It is pretty tricky; the crowds thin out to just a few brave souls. It is a great adventure, and we work up an appetite for our lunch of fresh grilled trout. The restaurant's dining areas are wooden platforms covered with Turkish rugs and pillows, set under the shade of lush trees and perched over the freshwater spring. After our long, lazy lunch, we visit the nearby ruins of Tlos and Xanthos with our stalwart group of six.

We avoid staying in the super-touristic places, particularly the ones that brag, "English Breakfast Served Here." We surely are not interested in a Turkish rendition of sausage, bacon, chips, and all that. The Germans have discovered this coast as well. Both the English and Germans love to lie on lounge chairs, toasting in the sun from morning till evening. When we see them at night sitting in the outdoor cafés, we can hear their voices, but all we can see are their white teeth and eyeballs.

Our laptop computer has been a blessing in these small towns. It has not been a problem hooking up through the pensions' phones—everyone has been most accommodating. There is access to the Internet via the cafés in most places, but going through Turkish telecom service to get to an Internet server can be difficult or impossible. I believe it's a bandwidth problem. They are just overloaded. The Internet is popular; even the Flower Pension here in Patara brags about having a website.

The Turkish language is unique but not terribly difficult. Michael and I have learned a few phrases, enough to get a smile from the people with whom we have contact. They love it and are quick to say, "Oh, you know Turkish!"

It's interesting how well we women can communicate, although we are barely able to speak each other's language. I get into long conversations with the women and then turn to Michael to give him the gist. He is absolutely amazed. It's no different in English. Men rarely understand, and women have a natural ability to communicate with each other in any country. It's as if the words are secondary.

Oops, another power outage. We experience about three a day here in Turkey. They are working on that problem, by the way, by building new dams throughout the country, no doubt all of them named "Atatürk."

Due to the large numbers of English and Germans, many of the Turkish men in the tourist villages marry foreign women. I'm not sure that this is a wise choice on the woman's part, based on what I have seen. In our drives through the countryside, I see the women bent over, working in the fields under the hot sun. Then they go back home to care for the children, feed the chickens, walk the cow, cook supper, clean house, wash and hang laundry, help run the family's restaurant, pension, or other secondary business, and take care of their mother-in-law. The men, on the other hand, stand by and watch the women do all the above, talk on their handy phones to impress each other, and after a hard day of supervising, spend the evening at the local tea house playing backgammon and schmoozing.

We have a chat with our waitress, Aysen, who is sixteen years old (she seems much older than that) and manages the café by herself at lunchtime. She was born and raised in Patara. We learn from her about the process of finding a husband and setting up home. First, she waits for her papa to receive a phone call from a local boy who says that he is interested in her. Then she can decide whether she wants to pursue this and will advise her papa accordingly. If she says okay, she will spend time getting to know him—maybe a year or two—but definitely not living with him, an absolute no-no in most of Turkey (other than the big cities, we are told).

Then, Aysen says, if they decide they will marry, the man will pay for the house and the woman will pay for the furnishings. After the wedding, they can move in together. On the rare occasion that the marriage fails, she takes back the furnishings. Unmarried women are frowned upon and are under tremendous social pressures outside of the larger cities. Aysen doesn't seem at all unhappy about her lot in life. She has no interest in attending college. She says the process for higher education takes about nine years and is expensive, and the chances of her landing gainful employment afterward are slim.

She says, "I would come back old and lazy, and unable to find work. That is what happened to my cousin."

I pick up a book in a local shop called *101 Questions Asked by Tourists about Turkey and Their Answers*, by Hakan Kutlu. In it, he explains, "Turkish people speak loud." Well, that's an understatement. Their conversational tone is equivalent to our shouting. I thought the Greeks had won that prize, but the Turks are strong contenders. We're told in this book that they don't mean any disrespect—they just are loud.

In a small village like Patara, I think that "handy phones" (cell phones) are totally unnecessary. Most people are just talking to their neighbors or spouses anyway, and they surely can be heard clear across town. My theory is that they've all gone deaf from listening to "Mambo Italiano." But the smiles and welcomes and good nature of the Turkish people make up for this. Even the children we pass in our car, or who pass us on their bicycles, will smile, say hello, and wave to us.

More notable quotables from *101 Questions* include discussing the low crime rates in Turkey. This book says, verbatim:

Question #86: What is the Theft and Crime Rate in Turkey? There is a strong public pressure against thieves, murderers, rapers (especially children abusers) in Turkey. When a thief spends a few years in the prison and is released, most of his relatives and neighbours will know it and will not talk to him. Rapers of young children are usually killed in prison by his cellmates, and when they have been questioned about what has happened, they all state that they do not know and have not seen anything. Drug dealers as well, they are not liked in the public and even not liked in the prison, prisoners think these people are poisoning their children outside and hard days wait for drug dealers in the prison and outside when they release by the public.

Who says they need to improve human rights in Turkey?
The author also addresses an all-important question as follows:

Question 58: Is chastity/virginity important for Turkish people? Virginity is still important for a large segment of the Turkish population. Especially in the East and Southeast regions of Turkey, virginity can be vital. Very few babies are born out of wedlock. Because of the limitations on sex before marriage, 48% of young men and 12% of young women masturbate.

* * *

Michael and I continue our eastward journey along the Mediterranean coast toward Kaş. The daytime sun is hot in July. Strenuous activities are out of the question, but a lounge in the shade is quite tolerable. We end up at a place called Kaş Camping, a little spot of heaven. The grounds, within walking distance from town, are well shaded and have a dock that reaches out beyond the rocky coast for a quick plunge into the most refreshingly clear blue water imaginable. We stay in a spotlessly clean bungalow.

There is a small gazebo-type café at the water's edge, and Argun, chef extraordinaire, prepares and serves our breakfasts, lunches, and snacks with style and savoir faire, always anticipating our needs. He seems pleased to have such an appreciative audience. Our daily entertainment includes watching a tortoise slowly work its way up a steep dirt road and amble into Argun's tiny kitchen area for its daily lunch treat (usually a whole tomato). Argun has been feeding this little guy for the past seven years. What a gentle, kind man he is.

The manager, Oscar, makes us feel like we are in a five-star resort instead of a campsite. One evening, we notice the Subaru's tire has a piece of metal sticking out of it and has gone flat. Oscar says, "Don't worry. Go have dinner, and Oscar will take care of everything."

Well, there isn't much we can do at this time of day anyway, so we willingly oblige. Early the next morning, Michael hears some noise outside of our bungalow. Sure enough, it is Oscar removing our tire. Michael goes back to sleep, and when we arise a couple of hours later the tire is fixed. Now, that's first-class service by anyone's standards.

A couple of days after Michael and I settle in, Rachel and her friend Meredith meet up with us as we had arranged through the magic of e-mail. They will be traveling with us for the next two weeks. We aren't surprised that they are ready to chill out and enjoy the hospitality of Kaş Camping after having traveled on buses for about twenty hours. We swim and snorkel every day.

One morning while snorkeling, I see a huge sea turtle lazily swimming beneath me, her green-and-brown coloring blending with the bottom about thirty feet below. I follow her, feeling an almost mystical, profound connection. I wonder where she has traveled, what she has seen, and in that moment I want desperately to continue swimming with her and take her journey wherever it may lead me. Eventually, I swim back to shore, where the gang is sprawled out on the sunbaked boulders. I share my experience, fully expecting them to be as enthusiastic as I am, but no—they are fairly sun-dazed and perhaps disbelieving. They pay little attention. Then, as I am looking out to sea, this beautiful creature pokes her huge head above the surface, perhaps to say good-bye to me before continuing on her journey alone.

The town of Kaş is lovely, a bit of the old and new combined. The waters have not yet been fished out, and many evenings in town we have grilled fish, delicious and reasonably priced. We also enjoy the large tea garden in the center of the town frequented by the locals.

We reluctantly leave Kaş after a week and travel onward to Olimpos. When we manage to fit in the extra backpacks and two more bodies, our little Subaru is loaded to the max. The air is dry and hot, so we can only travel about three hours at a stretch without either the car or us overheating. The main highway is excellent, and there's not much traffic—a good thing because Turks drive fast. The roads are steep with hairpin turns, but looking out the window we catch glimpses of the inviting turquoise-blue water. At one point, we just pull over, and all four of us hike down a steep cliff, don our suits, and plunge in. Oh, yes—much better!

We arrive at Olimpos, famous for its treehouses, ruins, beautiful beaches, and Australians and parties (one always seems to go with the other). This area of Turkey has steep mountains with thick pine forests and acres of orchards in the valleys with rocky gorges. The treehouses at our pension, called Caretta Caretta, appear reasonably sound as far as treehouses go, and we share the grounds with what seems like a thousand chickens nesting at night in the trees. They create quite a commotion at sunrise. The mile walk to the beach is extraordinary, through what used to be an important Lycian city from the second century BC. Scattered among the oleander and fig trees, along a stream of fresh mountain water, the fragmentary ruins sit. Beyond that, more ruins are carved into the steep cliffs overlooking the sea.

In the late afternoon, our fearsome foursome hikes several hours to the legendary mountain of Chimera. Natural gas escapes from the mountain, which creates eternal flames that blaze out of the rock crevices. There is one lonely vendor selling hot dogs cooked in the flames. As we take in this phenomenon, the full moon is coming up over the hills, and Meredith sings "Amazing Grace" in her clear, beautiful voice, which makes the evening even more magical.

We travel onward on our journey to Cappadocia in the center of Turkey and make an overnight stop in Eğirdir (pronounced "airdeer") in what's known as the lakes region of Turkey. We're heading north from the coast, ascending high into the mountains. As the weather gets cooler, the wildflowers get more profuse, and then a green-blue lake appears before us with the mountains in the background framing it. This looks like Switzerland! We stay the night in a pension run by a Turkish couple who spends part of the evening showing us the family album while we eat delicious fish stew.

The island had been inhabited by the Greeks until the Population Exchange in 1923, as evidenced by the crumbling Greek-style stone houses. The 1923 Population Exchange between Greece and Turkey was based upon religious identity and involved the Greek Orthodox citizens of Turkey and the Muslim citizens of Greece. It resulted in an agreed mutual expulsion. Our host tells us that just this year, since relations with Greece have improved slightly, a small group of elderly Greeks tearfully returned to visit their former homes in Eğirdir.

The last stop before Cappadocia is Sultanhani. This village's claim to fame is its Seljuk *caravanserei* (a large, fortified way station for caravans), built in 1229. I think they must have announced our arrival on the town crier's speaker because we no sooner unpack at our pension (one of two in town) than the children are lined up outside to take a look at the Americans. We enjoy their hospitality, their happy, smiling faces, and walking with them hand in hand throughout the village. We are led by a little boy into his home, and the mother immediately begins preparing *gözleme*, which she serves with tea, tomatoes, and cucumbers, and soon enough there are about thirty friends and neighbors crammed in and around the little stone dwelling. A couple of the kids know a smattering of English—Michael Jackson (always mentioned when Michael tells them his name) and the ubiquitous Bill Clinton.

The Turks love Bill Clinton. He is famous here for two things: he visited here and spoke a couple of words in Turkish, and he screwed around with Monica Lewinsky, which these village kids think is cool, judging by their giggles and hand motions when they mention her name. The village is picture-perfect, with its stone and stucco-type homes topped with thatched roofs of mud and grass; cows wander around freely, with no one paying any attention. Gaggles of geese waddle across the dirt roads; horse-drawn buggies serve as the main method of transportation. Everyone is friendly and smiling. What a special place to come upon by chance. To be able to share it with Rachel makes it even more so.

* * *

We arrive in Cappadocia the last week of June, a month after leaving Içmeler. The nights are cold enough to need a warm blanket. The days are hot (very hot) and dry, but the shade is comfortable. What a unique landscape: valleys filled with whimsical-looking rock formations. Many layers of volcanic ash have been compressed into *tufa* rock that slowly eroded to form what are called Fairy Chimneys above the ground. The *tufa* has also been carved to create churches, monasteries, houses, and storage both below ground and above. Love Valley (more familiarly known as Dick Valley) has giant formations that are obviously phallic in appearance, a popular hiking trail for creative photographers. There are large underground villages throughout the area. In the distance, we can see snowcapped volcanic mountains, the valleys covered with grassy fields and wildflowers.

Michael and I, along with Rachel and Meridith, stay in a pension in Göreme for the first few days. Rachel, Meredith, and I go for a sunset horseback ride with Mustafa, our tour guide, real estate agent, horseback guide, and just about anything else we might desire. Two dogs from the stables eagerly tag along. We ride in the valleys of this moonscape and pass by ancient Hittite cave dwellings, which were later adapted by the Christians for monasteries. The rose-colored sunset is exceptionally beautiful, and all is peaceful and serene when suddenly the dogs take off like a shot up into the mountains, barking and growling. Soon we see one of the dogs hurling a fox down the steep edge of a rock mountain, chasing after it at lightning speed. Chalk one up for the dogs—one pretty fox, dead as a doornail. Once we get over the initial shock, we have to realize that this wild habitat is also part of Turkey. We're not in Coral Gables anymore!

After two weeks, the girls leave to travel on their own for a while, and Michael and I decide to find a place we can rent for the next month or so. Mustafa takes it upon himself to help us with this mission. He grew up in Göreme, so he has many family members in town and knows virtually everyone—not surprising. Most families stay in these villages for several generations. So our quest begins.

My requirements for interior décor have greatly changed since the Coral Gables days. In fact, Michael wishes I had more discerning taste. Okay, so maybe the loft above the stables is a bit smelly, but it's definitely roomy. And I love being close to the horses, but we keep looking. We walk up a steep hill heading away from the center of town on a dirt road, making way for chickens, roosters, horse-and-buggies, wandering cows, and goats, to a tiny little house with a grand view of the valley. This has potential, but we have to roust up Mustafa's uncle to find the keys, and the front door has been hammered shut for the past umpteen years. No problem. We find an alternate path going up from rooftop to rooftop, and at last we are there. We walk past the outhouse (Turkish style—complete with treads) and finally get into the house from the roof access.

Mustafa assures us that he will put in a system so we will have hot water, and also that he will remove all the boxes and junk currently being stored in there. I'm already imagining where I'm going to put my stuff and how to fix up the place. Michael gets no farther than the Turkish-style outhouse but indulges me for the next half-hour. When he realizes I am quite serious about the possibility of renting it for the month, he says ever-so-diplomatically, "Let's continue looking."

We are shown yet another dwelling a few doors up the hill, but after a lengthy conversation between Mustafa and a lovely Turkish woman, we are told it was rented to a lady who writes for *Lonely Planet*. We look at a couple of more holes in the wall (cave dwellings) and then call it a day. Mustafa is going to have a family powwow and see what else might be available. He is seriously thinking of relocating his mother, but we put a stop to that one.

We follow another lead from a merchant in town and find the perfect cave pension/apartment in a little village called Uçhisar, a few minutes away from Göreme. The entire village is built in the volcanic mountain, visible for miles. The homes, stables, and pensions are carved into the soft *tufa* rock with windows that peep out everywhere, making the whole mountain look like something out of a Disney movie—vastly different from anything we've ever seen but typical of the entire Cappadocia region.

A steep cobblestone mixture of roads, tunnels, and alleyways connect and lead into the small but well-planned center of the village. The view from this perch is extraordinary. In the near distance, there are mountain trails and a roadway with more donkey carts and horses than motor traffic. Our cave, with its natural air conditioning, is large and has a modern bathroom. There is a kitchen in a separate cave room below ours. The young couple who live here and manage it, Sinan and Demet, are from Istanbul, and Sinan speaks perfect English. We decide to call it home for the next several weeks.

In the morning as I sip my coffee, I watch the goings-on. So far today I've seen two camels, one herd of sheep and goats, and three horse-drawn buggies. We have the best view for the famous Cappadocian sunsets right from our terrace. And if that isn't enough, they have a lounge area with Internet. All this for only US$225 per month. We have immersed ourselves in Cappadocia. It feels good to unpack and settle in after being on the road for the past month.

Sherifeh—a toast to being nomad cave dwellers!

∗ ∗ ∗

Michael and I leave for a two-day camping/trekking trip in Aladağlar National Park in the Taurus Mountains, a couple of hours' drive south of Cappadocia. This is the mountain range that begins in Turkey and extends into India and Nepal (becoming the Himalayas). When we are invited to join this expedition by some new acquaintances in town, we have no idea what to expect. We think it is just an excuse for a party out in the woods somewhere, and we're like, "Sure, why not?"

It is indeed a party and in the woods, but so much more as well. Greg is an Irishman currently living in the area and is a professional Alpine guide. He is a font of information on life in this region, and we learn about how the nomads live in the highlands and cope with the dramatic changes in season, about the animals and plant life that inhabit them, and he entertains us the entire time with his Irish humor and storytelling skills. There are thirteen of us. The average age is about twenty-eight (not factoring in our ages), and it's a veritable potpourri of people. Some are living here, and others just passing through—all wonderfully compatible and fun.

The mountain scrambling we do shortly after we arrive is a good warmup. We satisfy our appetites with a dinner of fresh grilled trout that we pick up from a trout farm on the way to the campsite, chicken, grilled peppers, and vegetable salad. After dinner, we sit around the campfire and share travel stories, with plenty of *raki*, of course.

We meet four huge dogs, a special breed indigenous to these mountains known as *karabaş* (pronounced "karabash"). They are beautiful creatures, with coloring similar to the local sheep—pale with thick fur and black muzzles. Although they are not totally domesticated, they cohabit with nomad families and protect their flocks from the frequent wolf attacks that occur, in exchange for some food. Greg tells us that sometimes the dogs' ears and tails are cut off to prevent the pack of wolves from grabbing hold of them and bringing them down for the kill. This group of dogs decided to stay in the valley and hang around because when campers are present they can enjoy chicken and fish and other leftovers. Bones? No problem. Two bites of their strong jaws, and they're ground to bone meal. The Turkish man who assists the trekking groups knows these dogs well and assures us they are quite harmless to humans, and they guard the campers during the night. We won't have to worry about the wolves, but venturing away from our tents into the woods to pee is a terrifying prospect.

We wake up early for breakfast and head off to climb the Taurus Mountains. *Okay, this we can handle,* I hope. We load our backpacks with water and sandwiches and trek along donkey paths through woods up above the forest line on a craggy granite mountain called Alaca. We stop often enough to let those who drank too much *raki* the night before catch their breath and those who think they are still twenty-eight rest their weary bones, and three and a half hours and 3,300 feet later we reach the peak, which is about 8,000 feet in elevation. We cross over to a plateau and take enough photos to compete with the Japanese tourists. The day is clear, with an incomparable view. We play in patches of snow and enjoy our sandwiches, feeling rather marvelous that we've made it this far. Thank God neither Michael nor I have to carry the watermelon.

We hike a bit farther up to another plateau along the ridge of the mountain and visit a nomad family that Greg knows well. We are generously offered Turkish tea and perform a little first aid in return. The mother has a badly infected finger. I have some Neosporin in my backpack, and a nurse in our group bandages the finger by placing flatbread soaked in hot water on it and then wrapping it with a dry cloth. Another family member complains that her eyes hurt, so I unpack my Visine. After demonstrating how it works, we apply it to her eyes. She asks if she can keep it, and of course I am glad to give it to her. We refill our water bottles from the ice-cold fresh spring water and continue on.

The trek down proves to be challenging, especially on legs that are a bit wonky from the climb, but we all make it without incident. By four o'clock in the afternoon we are back at the camp. The two days were well organized—truly an experience we were lucky to be a part of. It feels so good to come home to our cave pension. We look forward to each and every day.

Turkey has wrapped her arms around us, and we are content to be held.

Downtown Göreme

Uchisar

Our pension, Uchisar

View from our pension

Love Valley

CHAPTER 19

Still in Turkey

A good traveler has no fixed plans and is not intent on arriving.

—Lao Tzu

Nearly three months have passed since we arrived in Turkey, and our visas are due to expire. They tell us we do not have to leave the country but can renew them with a translator in the government offices in Nevşehir, a town only a short distance from where we are currently living, in Uçhisar. So we bring Sinan and Demet, who have become good friends.

On the first trip, we learn the exact documentation that is needed in order to renew our visas. The next visit began "the process," kind of a Keystone Cops scavenger hunt, to find the right office for a signature. When you find the right one, you are given the next clue. After getting several signatures from various offices in the three-story government building, which has no elevator, we need signatures from offices in the police department, located in a different four-story building. We—that is, Michael—have to submit to an interview with the office of the governor's aide to make sure he is a stand-up character. I grow a little worried during this part. He is in there for the longest time. People come and go from the office, but there is no sign of Michael. Lines extend out into the hallway, and the secretary becomes frantic because appointments are by then backed up. But still no Michael. Then I notice çay being brought in—clearly, Michael is in full schmooze. Sinan, Demet, and I settle in for the wait. At last, the door opens to the sound of laughter, and they release him. As it turns out, the governor's aide spent two years in Ft. Lauderdale and enjoyed conversing with Michael in English.

We just need a few more signatures, but lunchtime starts and everything shuts down for a couple of hours. After lunch, we hand over the signed papers and money. The police officer inserts a form into her manual typewriter with five carbon copies (the computer behind her was just for show). We're so close now … when we are informed, "We have to process the paperwork. Come back in two days."

I just came along for the fun of it anyway. I don't need to sign a thing; nobody needs to meet me. I'm strictly chattel. This is Turkey. Like lots of other places in the world, I'm afraid.

The weather is hot and dry in midsummer, but inside our carved *tufa* cave room, it's cool to the point where we need blankets. We are eager to explore other parts of this fascinating country and will head for the Black Sea coast and the mountains just south of there. After one last night of playing a game of Hearts and drinking *raki* with Sinan and Demet, we say our good-byes and exchange e-mail addresses.

Our first day out, we drive a few hours north on a decent rural road and pull over for a moment to consult our map and discuss which town to hole up in for the night. A man appears out of nowhere to ask if he might help us out, but of course he speaks no English. We ask for a *pensiyon.* He nods vigorously, points west, and says, "Sorgun." We locate it on our map and see a town about a mile down the road. He says "*Çok güzel,*" or very beautiful, one of the few Turkish words we know.

We confidently head for Sorgun. Once there, we drive on a dusty cobbled road into town and can't find anything that looks like a pension and certainly nothing *çok güzel.* We are a bit road-weary by now and loop back around and come upon the police station.

Michael goes in and I stay in the car since I am wearing shorts and a tank top. I feel inappropriately dressed, even though the temperature is well into the nineties. A few minutes later, a policeman comes to the car window and invites me to come in and join him and Michael for *çay.* I grab a long-sleeved blouse, slip a long cotton skirt over my shorts, and follow him in. We understand that the chief is on his way and speaks English, so we drink tea and wait. The chief arrives. We immediately relax and have a delightful chat. He lived in Los Angeles for a while, working in security for the Turkish Embassy. He explains to us that he and his family are on their way to his son's circumcision, and as soon as that is done he'll come back and escort us to a nice hotel. We are introduced to the family—his wife and three kids, including his eleven-year-old son, who is soon to be circumcised. The plan is to rendezvous at the police station in an hour or so.

In Islamic Turkey, circumcision is much more than a surgical procedure. Traditionally performed between the ages of five and twelve, it's seen as the first landmark in the boy's religious life, proof that he is strong, brave, and ready to be called a man. To this end, the procedure is generally performed with a local anesthesia but sometimes with none at all, as the pain is an integral part of the ritual. In the festivities surrounding the circumcision, the boy is made to wear a king's costume, and the assembled family and friends shower him with gifts and tie gold coins to his belt. Almost 30 percent of Turkish parents choose the traditional method over the postnatal procedure in hospitals, and in rural Turkey up to 85 percent of circumcisions are performed without any doctor at all. A boy who will be circumcised is called *sünnet çocuğu* (child of circumcision).

The police chief is white as a ghost when he returns to his office and confesses that he is still shaken. His son is carried past the lineup of cheering and clapping policemen, wrapped up in a white sheet, into the chief's apartment behind the police station. The chief asks us to follow him in his patrol car, and we drive a couple of miles and pull up to a hotel.

The chief negotiates the price for us, which comes to a grand total of 12 million lira a night, including breakfast (about US$17). We are delighted just to have a place to sleep for the night, but as it turns out, the hotel is sort of a spa, with natural hot thermal spring water throughout the entire facility—including in our own bathtub. I hadn't seen a bathtub in, like, *forever*, and I luxuriated in a hot soak for about an hour. We are surprised that even the water in the toilet was hot thermal spring water, which is naturally about sixty degrees Celsius (close to boiling). Michael was a little worried about boiling his balls.

Afterward, we go to the owner, and after playing a complicated game of charades he finally figures out that we are hungry and want to find a place to eat. He leads us by hand out the door to our car and gets in with us, and off we go. A few minutes later, we reach his destination. The hotel owner has a few words with the restaurant owner, after which we are comfortably seated. We fully expect the hotel owner to have dinner with us, but he excuses himself and leaves. Within minutes, we are brought an absolutely delicious meal, complete with lentil soup, salad, *caçik* (cold yogurt soup with cucumbers), grilled chicken and quail, and a sweet baklava for dessert. When we return to the hotel, the police chief is waiting for us to make sure everything is satisfactory. What an incredible experience. This is the Turkey we love and can't yet leave.

Amasya is the next stop in our journey to the Black Sea. Amasya is an ancient city nestled in a valley with Ottoman houses built alongside a river. It is referred to as the Venice of Turkey. Michael and I are walking through the town, admiring a 700-year-old *hamam* (Turkish bath), when a man introduces himself to us in English and asks us if we have any questions. Vadet, a schoolteacher, walks with us for a while and then invites us to have tea. As is typical in Turkey, he is pleased to share his town and his culture with us. He takes it upon himself to make sure we don't miss a single fortress, tomb, or mosque. We walk with him to his apartment, where he introduces us to his wife and two teenage daughters, and we have a glass of *ayran*.

Ayran is a blend of sour yogurt, water, and a pinch of salt, and it tastes better than anything else in the world when it's broiling hot outside (and inside—air conditioning is nonexistent in these villages). The Turks drink this regularly and claim it is good for a variety of ailments and keeps them healthy. It's a good thing indeed because the last thing you want is to get sick in Turkey.

He invites us to join him at his favorite teahouse to play *Okey*, a game kind of like gin rummy but with tiles. The men often play this game in the teahouses throughout Turkey. I think the women must play as well, but never in public. I am surprised when Vadet invites Michael and me into a teahouse. I am the only female in the place, but they make exceptions for foreigners who enter with a Turkish friend. We get a foursome together, are served Turkish tea, and with several men coaching me from the sidelines I proceed to win quite handily. What fun! We spend the rest of the day with Vadet, and through him we are ready to appreciate the splendor of Amasya.

✵ ✵ ✵

We stay in a beautifully reconstructed Ottoman house with bright, spacious rooms and modern plumbing (meaning a toilet that flushes and a hook on the wall for the showerhead). We befriend a young American man who is in Amasya doing research for *Fodor's Travel*

Guide. He becomes ill the next day, and they tell us he has been sent to the hospital. Michael and I think we'll pay him a visit, and we go with Vadet. The public hospital is a nightmare. It is so hot you can hardly breathe. There is no reception or information desk to find out about patients either. While we stand around in the emergency room, we are witnesses to ghastly sights—blood on the floor, someone vomiting and calling for help. People are in close quarters and in complete disarray. We stop to ask a doctor if he has seen a young American man, and he informs us that he has been released from the hospital. We find him back at the pension, having been given an IV and medications at the hospital. We've heard numerous stories throughout our travels in Turkey from expats about the sorry state of the medical profession. We're told some of the private hospitals are better, but I surely don't want to find out. I've been known to drink six glasses of *ayran* a day!

After leaving Amasya, we finally reach Samsun, our first town on the Black Sea coast. It is a great disappointment. The one and only highway that stretches all along the northern coast is in disrepair, and the drivers pass like maniacs all over the place. It is a challenge to stay alive, and the nasty-looking coastline is littered with trash. The water is polluted, so even though it's hot and muggy, we don't dare go swimming. We do not stop in Samsun but continue heading east. We are anxious to check our e-mail, and in an unlikely-looking village along the coast, we find a small Internet café. We check our mail and are served tea, and they refuse to take any money from us. Our spirits buoyed, we are ready to continue on.

After an overnight stay in Ünye, we continue heading east to Trabzon, a city on the Black Sea coast just a few miles west of Georgia. Trabzon is fun—fairly cosmopolitan, with lovely tea gardens in the center of town. The following morning, we head inland. Within fifteen minutes of leaving the hot, muggy coast, a different world opens up, much more to our liking. The pictures in our Black Sea guidebook do not do it justice. The steep mountains are completely carpeted with thickly planted tea bushes, green meadows, and pine trees; the whole area is lush and beautiful. The temperature is refreshingly cooler. We breathe a sigh of relief as we sight the large wooden homes high up in the mountains for which this area is known. A pulley system rigged up from the road transfers everything up and down from the houses. The people of this area (the Hemşin and the Las) wear colorful scarves and clothing indicating the exact region in which they live. We see women working on the slopes cutting the tea plants.

We stay briefly in Sumela, the highlights of which were the grilled trout (*alabalik*) that we ate for six meals in a row; the dessert typical of this region called *sutlach*, like rice pudding but with less rice and sweeter; and our visit to the Sumela Monasteri, which clings to a sheer rock wall high above evergreen forests.

We then drive to Uzungöl, located in a valley beside a small lake with a huge mosque reflected in it, between mountains that visitors and residents of Turkey say compare to the Swiss Alps. Rachel, after having seen Meredith off in Istanbul, joined up with a family friend, Alex. We rendezvous in Uzungöl to spend a few days all together.

Uzungöl ("long lake") was built as a tourist destination for Turkish families. Most of the women visitors wear scarves covering their hair, long skirts, and overcoats. We hear no English spoken at all. The town itself is nothing special, but the people make it special for us. In the evenings, we watch traditional Turkish dances performed by the men, although in one of the less conservative hotels the women did join in as the evening progressed. We are fortunate to meet a lovely Turkish couple from Ankara. Mehmet, a career Army officer, and his wife, Ayshagul, both of whom speak English, explain the meaning behind some of the dances, the music, and the different instruments used. We learn much from our new Turkish acquaintances about the traditions, customs, and close-knit family ties of the Turkish people, and we are able to see what most tourists could not encounter on a short visit to this country.

On one of our outings, Rachel, Alex, Michael, and I pile into the Subaru and take a drive on the one (and only) pitted, rocky dirt road out past Uzungöl, which slowly works its way up the forested mountains and alongside a rapidly rushing creek. Up, up, and still up this road we go. We are relishing the cool and misty weather.

After an hour, we make it above the treeline, and the vista opens before our eyes. We reach the *yayla*. Nomadic herdsmen of Turic origin used to call their herding locations by different names depending on the season. *Yazlak, yaylak, güzlek,* and *kışlak* refer to herding locations of different seasons of the year. But out of the four, *yayla* and *kışla* (with the last letter dropped) are more widespread. *Kışla* (from *kış*, meaning winter) refers to relatively warmer places in the plains, and *yayla* refers to mountain slopes where the pasturing is easier during the summer. It seems as if the rolling hills go on forever. There are pastures with cows grazing, wheat growing, and tiny villages with old wooden homes clustered together. Our Turkish travel handbook, called *Karadeniz* (Black Sea), says, "The *yayla* smell—a mixture of wet grass, cow dung, and sooty firewood—is the most unmistakable of all Black Sea sensory experiences. A traveler who hasn't smelled it cannot really say he has been to the Black Sea. A traveler who has is likely to come back for more."

We feel inspired by this place in a way none of us could have imagined. We stumble upon a family on their lunch break from work in the field. They ask us to join them and share their lunch—hot *gözleme* (a savory Turkish flatbread) and crumbly flavor-bursting cheese, fresh tomatoes, and hot tea from a thermos. We don't want to eat too much of their food, but they are insistent, and none of our bunch is able to refuse food anyway. We establish the relationships of our new acquaintances— the man, with whom we communicate in German, his wife, her sister, and two grown children, all working as an efficient team threshing and baling the hay. Throughout these hills, families work together to do the same thing at this time of year.

After lunch, the women pop up and start back to work. Rachel and I figure they will probably appreciate a little help, so we walk with them to a pile of hay and watch them at first. Here's how it works—one woman stands inside a wood-plank box, which is about three feet wide and about five feet high. The other women put in armfuls of hay, and the one in the box stomps it down. The process continues until the box is full, and she stands atop of the packed-down hay. A couple of wires are then twisted to tie up the bale. She opens one side of the box and pushes it out. She jumps down, and two ropes are tied around the bale. One woman then crouches down and hefts the bale on her back, strings the rope around her shoulders, and walks it (still in a crouch) to where the other bales are stacked a few meters away and, of course, uphill. Simple, yes, but efficient, and you don't use any gasoline.

I don't want these mountain folk to think we American women are weaklings, so I volunteer to carry one of those bales of hay over to the pile. They are laughing with glee while I try to find the right balance in a bent-over position with a humongous bale on my back. A couple of quick steps this way … a few more corrective steps that way … I think I've got it now and am able to walk it over to the pile. No problem!

Several minutes later, when I am finally able to straighten up again, I think, *I am woman. I am strong!* What I didn't know was that one of the women was behind me lifting the weight of the bale off my back so that I could do this. It's all about teamwork. And humility. We say our good-byes and leave with wonderful memories (and lots of hay in my bra), intoxicated by the *yayla* smell.

After a few days, we leave Uzungöl, and Rachel and Alex go on to Istanbul. Rachel finishes her incredible summer journeys and heads back to the United States and school, while Alex continues his travels in Turkey for a while before heading to Africa, which he is determined to explore. These young people have a great sense of adventure, and they create their opportunities. I am trying to imagine what my mother and father would say if I'd have said, "Hey, folks. I think I'll just hop on a plane and travel somewhere for some period of time in some exotic place by myself!"

They'd probably have given me a couple of aspirin and an enema and sent me to my room.

Michael and I travel farther into the Kaçkar Dağlari mountain range in the northeast part of Turkey to Camlihemşin. The highlights of this trip are our pension in Senyuva, located right smack on the edge of a river deep in the woods, and sleeping to the sound of rushing water; our two-hour hike up a steep mountain to the Zilkale (castle); our day's walk up to another *yayla* called Ortan and being invited by a local to have tea and cornbread; the picturesque village of Ayder and beyond, where we encounter an honest-to-goodness glacier that formed a natural bridge over a river, which we walk across to have our picnic lunch of fresh peaches and cheese; and fording streams that cross the dirt roads on which we always seem to venture with our Subaru. It is incredible how much water there is in this part of the country.

Life in this mountain area seems to have remained the same throughout time, apparently unaffected by technology. It is such a dramatic change from the touristy Mediterranean and Aegean coasts. Our three weeks here greatly enrich our knowledge and love of this country.

* * *

At last, we head back toward the northern coast to Rize to meet the ferry that will bring us west to Istanbul in two days—a great way to avoid having to drive on that awful coastal road again. Every street corner in Rize has vendors selling fresh produce. Outstanding peaches, fresh ripened figs, sweet green grapes, and melons are in season. Rize is famous worldwide for its tea; we enjoy drinking it and eating in the one of the many *kafeterias*. The real Turks eat in the *kafeterias*, and any women and children who come into a *kafeteria* immediately go upstairs so as not to be seen. Only the men (and me—I'm excused because I'm a foreigner and people figure I don't know any better) eat downstairs. It works perfectly for us because you can just go where the warm fresh food is kept on display and simply point to what you want; there's nothing better when you're tired and hungry and your Turkish is sorely lacking.

The waiters here understand what fast food is all about. The bread is already on the table before we sit down. Then our selection is brought to us just as we get settled in our chairs. It's good, and it's cheap. As soon as I bring the last forkful of food to my mouth, the waiter swoops in and takes the plate away. Watching the Turkish men eat is a sight—bread in one hand, fork in the other, face hovering over the plate, shoveling in the food so fast you can't even see what they're eating. As soon as the plates are taken, they pop up from their seats and are gone. No leisurely conversation. Truth be known, I'm all for it. I'm always finished eating before Michael. He's started to catch on, though, and has begun shoveling his food in true Turkish style. I think we had better unlearn some of this before we return to Italy.

On the ferry to Istanbul, we meet two American couples, both of which have lived in Istanbul for many years. We are drawn to each other like magnets. While they catch up on American movies, politics, and business, we are curious to find out what it is like to live, work, and raise children in Turkey. We enjoy their company tremendously, and it juices up an otherwise lackluster ferry ride. The ferryboat is rocking and rolling and is pretty rough, but we manage to pool our snacks and drinks, sit together at a table on the deck, and continue our conversation throughout the evening. Other people on the ferry are leaning over the sides, barfing their guts out. When we order sodas from the bar, the bartender asks, "Don't Americans get seasick?" We all think that is pretty funny and confirm his belief. "Nah, we're tough," we tell him. But I pay for my arrogance later in the privacy of my cabin. I think the Pringles did me in.

We say our farewells in Istanbul, and now Michael and I are ready to be road warriors instead of sea(sick) farers.

Our next destination is Gallipoli.

* * *

We begin by catching up on history at the museum and walking the grounds of the 1915 battlefields of Gallipoli (*Gelibolu* in Turkish). It is an eerie feeling to stand at the site where almost half a million soldiers lost their lives. Atatürk, the founder of modern Turkey, built a memorial at Anzac Cove to honor the soldiers. His words were poignant.

> These heroes that shed their blood and lost their lives … you are now lying in the soil of a friendly country. Therefore rest in peace. There is no difference between the Johnnies (Anzacs) and the Mehmets (Turks) to us where they lie side by side here in this country of ours … You the mothers who sent their sons from faraway countries, wipe away your tears; your sons are now lying in our bosom and are in peace. After having lost their lives on this land, they have become our sons as well.

After Gallipoli, we drive in a southerly direction along the Aegean coast. We spend the night in a tiny rural farming village called Tevfikiye, just outside the gates of Troy. Troy is on the edge of the Aegean Sea and the Dardanelles. We find a decent little pension that offers the basics, just a short walk from the town center; we figure we'll at least get a good night's sleep. After a tasty meal in a café in town, we begin to hear music and drumbeats and notice throngs of people—some carrying chairs, some carrying trays of food—walking in the direction of … our pension. We walk back, dodging tractors, donkeys, and just about any and all forms of transportation. We had no idea this place has so many people! What the heck is going on here?

We soon solve the mystery; one of the village's young boys is having his circumcision party, and the entire population of this village has come to celebrate. The young boy leads the parade, riding on a small white pony in the traditional white satin suit with spangled hat and red satin sash. We follow along on the unpaved roads past old barnyards with cows mooing, gaggles of geese scurrying around to avoid the crowd, the loud squawking of hens and roosters, and of course the cats and dogs. The party is culminating at the end of our block. In Turkey, you never know quite what to expect. It is a great evening—but not for sleeping. We enjoy walking around the ruins of Troy, which are well-marked with explanatory signs, and take pictures of the huge replica of the wooden Trojan horse. It is amazing to stand on this hilltop and gaze at some of the oldest walls in the world, still standing. They were built around Homer's time (circa 800 BC). And I thought our Coral Gables house built in AD 1926 was old.

* * *

After all this history, we need to eat, drink, and be merry. We find it all in Ayvalik, which used to be an old Greek village and is now a lively, popular seaside town. Michael and I spend a week in Ayvalik and enjoy dips in the Aegean, sunset drinks on a deck that juts out over the water with a view of the Greek Island of Chios, and a ferry excursion to Alibey Adasi, a small island a few minutes off the coast, for a lunch of fresh fish.

We find a clothing store, and Michael buys some desperately needed new shirts to enhance his sparse wardrobe. I buy several as well—taking advantage of the cheap prices before we head back to Europe. Boy, are we going to miss all this when we leave Turkey … but I can't think about that now.

We drive south to Selçuk to visit the ancient ruins of Ephesus, where we encounter a little excitement. We are robbed! Our car window is smashed, and they grab Michael's small suitcase. We are so lucky that they don't take the computer or any of the other bags that are in the car. The only things in the stolen bag are Michael's underwear, some well-worn shirts, and sadly the new clothes he just bought. Evidently this doesn't happen often. The police are apologetic and helpful, which takes the sting out of the incident. They even escort us to a repair shop so the window can be fixed—a whopping US$22. We have since replaced most items by shopping at the local markets: four Lacoste shirts (the "good" fakes, we are told) at US$5 apiece and men's underwear (one color, one style—that's all they have in Turkey) at US$1.75 a pair. It would have been helpful to know the word for "underpants" in Turkish so Michael wouldn't have had to drop his pants. Now Michael looks more Turkish than ever. The men here love him and insist that he must be Turkish.

* * *

It's September, and we are back in Içmeler, where our return trip in Turkey began four months ago. The tourists are here in full force; we much prefer it preseason. We've visited with some friends, caught up on e-mails and laundry, and will stop at a few more must-see sights on the way out of town, including Pamukkale, Hieropolis, and Aphrodisias. In a few days, we will take a ferryboat out of Çesme, Turkey, and head straight for Brindisi, Italy.

As luck would have it, the 2,000-year-old amphitheater in Ephesus is hosting a piano concert our last night in Turkey. It is a clear, picture-perfect evening spent sitting on the ancient stone benches under the moon and the stars, mesmerized by the mystical ambiance as we listen to classical music in the natural acoustics of the theater. We watch the native cats slither in and out of the ancient stones and across the stage as if they own the place, which of course they do. What a grand finale for our visit.

We have been fulfilled and enriched by the people and the landscapes of this fascinating country. We have thousands of pictures and many stories and must now venture on in true Gerber nomad fashion. The Turks have failed in only one way—they could not sell us a Turkish rug, try though they did. It's a good excuse for us to come back.

I guess you could say we are "wrapping up the turkey leg" of our trip!

* * *

Our travels around Turkey clearly demonstrate that it is a land of contrasts and contradictions:

Living in a cave—wired for the Internet.

A horse attached to a wagon drinking from a water fountain in front of a car rental place.

Old-fashioned barbershops, still offering a shave and a haircut, burning the hair off men's ears with a Bic lighter.

Fields being plowed with donkeys next to ones using tractors.

Main thoroughfares with trucks, buses, and horse-drawn wagons.

Muezzin prayer calls mixing with American pop music resounding in the streets.

Satellite dishes atop centuries-old stone houses.

Turkish women in traditional garb (baggy trousers and long-sleeved baggy blouses, lower half of face and head covered with white scarf) riding in the backs of horse-drawn carts, passing scantily clad female tourists on the back of motor scooters.

Turkish family in a one-room stone house playing Alanis Morrisette.

Muezzin calling men to pray in mosques, while would-be prayer-goers are reading newspapers with naked women on the cover.

Guarding the ruins, Patara

Families and their rugs for sale

Taking a break, Black Sea Region

Out for a stroll

CHAPTER 20

Return to Switzerland via Italy

We have no destinies other than those we forge ourselves.

—Jean-Paul Sartre

We had arranged with Holk and Margrith to be back in Switzerland in time to house-sit so they can go about their traveling, as planned earlier last summer. We'll be selling the Subaru in Switzerland a little over a year after we bought it in Zurich, which gives us about two weeks to spend in Italy.

Our departure from Turkey is timed in order to miss the busy tourist season in Italy, just as the weather is cooling off. We board our ferryboat from Çeşme, Turkey, on September 4 and land two days later in Brindisi, Italy. Having seen the major cities on our two previous visits to Italy during the past year and a half, we plan a different route this time. The ferry brings us to the heel of the Italian boot, which leaves about 800 miles to drive to reach Interlaken, Switzerland. Since our odometer broke about a year ago, I have no idea just how many miles we've put on our little Subaru, but this last stretch will surely be a challenge for it. The boat ride goes smoothly. From Brindisi, we head south for a short drive along the eastern coast to an elegant little town called Lecce, known for its baroque architecture. Our nostrils lead us into the Three Musketeers restaurant, where they take pity on us and let us in a half hour before their scheduled opening for lunch—we neglected to change our watches back an hour. We feast on a five-course meal, and our craving for Italian food is satisfied (for the moment).

Ready to put a few miles behind us, we turn west and drive along the arch of the boot, past miles and miles of vineyards chock full of large ripe purple grapes and orchards of olive trees. We follow signs for

San Marco Agriturismo campgrounds (serving breakfast and dinner) in Metaponto. It is set on a beautiful hillside farm under a cluster of trees, overlooking acres of fertile land. We are happy to be outdoors after being cooped up on the ferryboat. After our usual lengthy discussion, we decide on the perfect location to set up our tent and are soon visited by two playful white furry puppies that become bothersome when they begin teething on our camping equipment. I walk them back to where their mammoth mother is chained up; she is wagging her tail, so I think she'll be pleased that her pups are back with her.

I misjudge the situation. Once she has her pups safely by her side, she turns around and sinks her teeth into my thigh. We are playing tug-of-war with my quadriceps, but once she loosens her grip, I am able to pull my leg away and leap back out of her reach. Fortunately, I am wearing safari pants that have a lined pocket just at the location where the dog bites me, but she still manages to puncture my leg in three spots, one of them quite deep.

I am a bit embarrassed, but we go to the main house, show the young lady my rapidly swelling and bloody leg, and ask for assistance. She is horrified and probably afraid that I am going to make trouble for her. I assure her that it was my own stupidity to approach a chained dog, and we just want a little reassurance that the dog isn't rabid. She assures us that the dog is current on her shots, and she insists on taking us into town to have a visit with their family doctor.

The father drives us to town, during which time we have a chance to converse with the charming daughter, who speaks English beautifully. I chatter nonstop because I don't want to think about all those horror stories we've heard about Italian doctors, like going in for a splinter and coming out without the affected appendage. We arrive at the office in downtown Metaponto, where if we were looking left instead of right we'd have missed it. Half a dozen elderly people are already waiting for the arrival of the doctor to open the clinic. Our hosts have some clout, and as the metal garage door leading to a one-room clinic is lifted up, we are ushered to the front of the line past some grumbling patients.

The doctor is pleasant. She treats the wounds with peroxide and iodine and decides that stitches are not needed to fix the three round holes in my thigh (amputation is also not needed). I am glad to hear that because the small, poorly lit room looks like a medical facility from the early 1900s, and I am not keen on having any of those instruments touch me. Our hostess is more relieved than I am and insists on paying for the antibiotic that is prescribed for me. Dinner that night makes up for the whole incident—our host really cooks up a storm, and after several glasses of the local red wine, I am feeling no pain.

* * *

Continuing our journey the next day, we drive deeper into the Basilicato region to the ancient city of Matera, which is famous for its stone cave dwellings, called *sassi*. These dwellings, some of which were inhabited up until about thirty years ago, are reminiscent of the cave dwellings in Cappadocia, Turkey. We walk through the entire village and visit some of the many rock churches, Byzantine and Romanesque, many with well-preserved frescoes. There are exquisite new homes being constructed along the perimeter, with a lively young professional population. We opt for a real bed and a good night's sleep, so we stay in a beautiful hotel overlooking the *sassi*. We find the people of this southern region to be particularly friendly and warm, and the cities are not as touristic as many others we've visited in Italy.

Our journey continues across to the magnificent Amalfi Coast and up to Naples and Pompeii. We walk (I limp) through the ruins, which are as dramatic as I expected and well worth seeing. We have sunny, cool, perfect weather for the entire trip.

Then we drive north to the Tuscany region and stay in Siena. The region is breathtaking, with its terracotta brick buildings surrounded by soft, curvy hills covered with trees, meadows, and vineyards. In the town, window-shopping is a treat. We lose ourselves in the maze of alleyways and enjoy the ambiance at every turn. After a couple of days of camping in Siena, we continue north and then stop to see the leaning tower of Pisa and take a nice stretch on the sprawling lawns of the piazza. The weather continues to be beautiful, and we drive along the western coast through Cinque Terre, a feast for the eyes. We could easily spend two years here just to begin to grasp the wonders of Italy, but we travel on, wanting to be certain we arrive in Switzerland in time for Holk and Margrith to begin their business trip.

Farther north along the highway, we enter Portofino with its gorgeous coastline, magnificent architecture, steep cliffs covered with ripe grapevines lush with fruit, and grand villas, elegant shops, and restaurants. *Oh, là là*—definitely for the rich and famous. We're neither, so we only stay for one glorious night in a four-star hotel, taking full advantage of those twenty-four hours. We have been camping for the past several days, so small pleasures are deeply appreciated. We are extolling the simple virtues of a bathtub with plenty of hot water and high pressure; soft sheets with thousands of threads per inch; thick, fluffy bath towels; watching CNN, but who really cares; and a view of the Italian Riviera. Oh yes, what a bit of luxury and shopping can do for the spirits!

Back down to earth (literally), we camp on the banks of Lake Maggiori for our last evening in Italy. Our struggling Subaru sounds worse every day, and we aren't sure we will make it over the Alps to get to Switzerland. But our car is like the *Little Engine That Could*. Ever so slowly, we climb up the Simplon Pass and into Switzerland. Ah! To be back in the land of snowcapped Alps, lush green carpeted meadows, perfectly groomed cows, large wooden barns, and Swiss chalets colorfully adorned with flowers. After months of hot, dry summer in Turkey, seeing Switzerland is like quenching a mighty big thirst with gallons of refreshing, cool mountain spring water. My body and spirit absorb the beauty of Switzerland and feel restored. There is just no place like it that we've ever been to, and I am so glad to be here once again.

When we arrive in Interlaken, Margrith and Holk have prepared a lovely welcome home dinner of *raclette* and all the fixings for us. The following day, we drive our minibus to Holk's Subaru dealership. Our mechanic, Lawrence, is amazed that the car he fixed up for us a year ago survived our long journey from Switzerland through Italy, Greece's mainland and islands, Israel, Turkey, and back again. He just stands there with his arms folded, shaking his head, saying, "I don't believe it." Well, believe it, 'cause we're back!

Holk has a young couple lined up to buy our minibus as soon as Lawrence can get it back in shape. After looking over the engine (cracked manifold, among other things), we realize how fortunate we are to have made it back. Our little Subaru was so much a part of our adventures, and its behavior determined many of our destinations. It is with mixed emotions that we sell it.

CHAPTER 21

Autumn in Switzerland

A journey like this suggests some kind of personal transformation, but I am not sure that people really change in their basic character. It is probably true that they simply become more intensely themselves, or what they were meant to be all along.

—Elisabeth Bumiller

We are just so Swiss now. We have a "SuperCard" from the local supermarket called the Co-op and a "Swiss Pass" for half-price fares for public transportation. We are quite proper about recycling garbage on the specified days and specified locations in the specified garbage bags filled with specified trash. We have a real scare when Michael neglects to flatten the cardboard egg container before throwing it in the trash, and I am still convinced we'll get a knock on our door and it'll be the garbage Nazis. Hopefully, if I whip out my Co-op SuperCard, they'll forgive us this one time.

The Swiss are in a class by themselves with regard to implementing and adhering to recycling programs. There's recycling for glass, and they go even further by separating the bottles by color—brown, green, and white. They have large recycling machines for crushing plastic bottles. The supermarkets do not provide free plastic bags; you need to bring your own sacks for carrying groceries. Outdoor composts are used where possible. Only regulation garbage bags are collected, and they are costly. In this way, you become much more conscious of recycling whatever is possible, putting the vegetable and table scraps in the compost, and flattening whatever you can to take up less room in the bag. Newspapers are bundled and put aside until the collections notice comes, and they are then picked up by children's organizations and recycled. There are strategically located dispensers of small plastic bags to use for cleaning up after your pets and receptacles for disposing of same. The Swiss dogs are so well trained that they've learned to poop directly into these bags, then twist them around and fling them directly into the receptacles! There is no need for hidden cameras, except maybe for a couple of Americans who might dare to disobey. It is so ingrained in the Swiss to always play by the rules, and there are thousands upon thousands of rules. The result? Phenomenal.

The day after we arrive in Interlaken, we watch the cows come home and parade right in front of our house, all to assure us that winter is not far away. The farmers bring their cows down off the high Alps and into the valleys in Swiss-style ceremonious fashion. They wear their traditional Swiss outfits: the men in *lederhosen* (German for breeches made of leather, which may be either short or knee-length) and the women in typical Swiss folk costume, which features a puffy blouse and skirt, a tight vest, and a generous use of ribbon or lace, often with beautiful floral embroidery. The cows wear their special enormous parade cowbells, the sound from which travels for miles. To top it off, the cows are adorned with fresh flower headpieces—the larger the bouquet, the more milk that cow produced in the past year. Can you imagine the conversation among the contestants?

"Moooove over, you big cow. This year, *I* am wearing the bonnet." "Your teats are a bit saggy this year, dear. Time for a nip and tuck."

I took so many pictures I thought Michael would have a cow. Enough bovine humor—but oh, we do have a full moooooon tonight!

We'll be using our Interlaken home as a base but plan to take a few more trips around Europe before we finish up with this part of the world. We head back to Venice to meet up with our friends from Miami, Nancy and Marty. This is our second visit, and I think it's even better than the first. We don't feel pressured to see the tourist sites and are able to be more selective in how to spend our time. The weather is superb. We are lucky—just a few days before we arrive, the entire region experienced severe flooding.

From Interlaken, the trip takes about ten hours by train (having to bypass those flooded areas), but we sleep, eat, and read. Venice is as magical as ever, and listening to concerts (Vivaldi and Bach) in the magnificent churches is extraordinary. The city is hosting a marathon, so it is packed with people from all over the world. We visit an exhibition of Modigliani and then Rodin. So we don't concentrate only on food, although we do have an outrageous *tagliatelle* with shrimp and tomatoes and pack up tons of prosciutto, provolone, and biscotti for the long train ride back.

Coming back to our chalet in Interlaken is heartwarming. The bells worn by cows grazing in the field right next to our chalet chime softly; Lisa the dog makes strange noises deep in her throat in her excitement at seeing us. We savor every minute of our time left in Switzerland. Every day on our walks, we are enthralled by the beauty of this place. It's such a treat for us to experience autumn after so many years in Florida. We walk through the woods on the well-marked paths, and our feet crunch leaves fallen from real, honest-to-goodness trees (not palms). We breathe in pine-scented fresh mountain air as we listen to the rushing water from creeks that seem to flow everywhere. We feast our eyes on the autumn Technicolor, able to live so much in the present moment.

Now that we're back in Switzerland, I have returned to my weekly meeting with the ladies of the English Club, also known as *Lesekränzli*. I am no longer a guest but an active, participating member. They have me reading German while they practice their English. I have so enjoyed spending time with my Swiss friends. I feel comfortable having open discussions with them about a number of topics and gain insight from their perspectives. It is a privilege to have had this short time together with them.

❊ ❊ ❊

Michael and I wake up to a clear, sunny, crispy-cool morning and decide to do the tourist thing and take the train to the top of the Jungfrau Mountain. It's a two-hour cog train ride to the lookout on the "Top of Europe" peak. The view is breathtaking (as is the altitude at 11,333 feet). We are fortunate to have a perfect day. The blue sky as the backdrop for the pure white glacial snow on the mountain peaks is spectacular, and we can see clear down and across to the valley of Interlaken. There are a couple of paragliders on a nearby peak, testing the wind to determine whether or not to fly down the mountain. Whew, what a fantastic ride that would be! I would do it. Yes, I believe I would. Now that I have had one tandem paragliding ride, I am experienced! I think it would actually be safer than downhill skiing—for me, at least.

In our daily lives, we're becoming experts at using public transportation. You can set your watch by the trains and the buses. "Always the same," as Holk would say.

It's oh-so-civilized. Buses are clean inside and out. Once you step on the bus, you are allowed precisely ten seconds to hand money to the overstressed bus driver, who must stay on schedule. We are just reaching the ten-second mark when Michael manages at last to get the money out of his pocket and handed over. A collective sigh of relief rises up from the passengers.

We eat most meals at home and buy just what we are sure we will consume, since prices are high. The food is packaged beautifully and is fresh, and we have a wonderful little kitchen complete with an oven (haven't had one of those for most of our trip), four burners (I only had one in Cappadocia, which was set on the top of a propane gas tank), pots, pans, and dishes—comfy and cozy. In any case, we haven't found any restaurants that are worth spending a lot of Swiss francs on. At least the dollar is strong at this time, which makes it a bit more comfortable for us to live here in Switzerland.

We've been traveling for close to two years now. The weather is getting cold. Holk and Margrith have returned from their travels, and so we are winding down our Swiss time and starting to think about going back to the United States with mixed emotions. Our investments took a hit when the tech stocks collapsed, and we need to work a few more years before we officially retire. *Arrgh*. We've become so adept at being footloose. So we will be going back "home," except we don't have a home! We have no car, and what's left of our furniture is in storage. Where to begin? This occasionally freaks me out, but I'm trying to look at things in a positive way. It will be so different for us now, a new beginning—we have no ties to a home, schools, or jobs and can begin anew. Maybe new careers in a new part of the country; anything is possible. It feels a little like it did when we graduated from school. We both have positive attitudes and figure we will make it work. Things always seem to have a way of falling into place. And in a few years we may be "Traveling without Reservations" again.

Chillin' in Venice

Watching the cows come home

Winter has arrived

AFTERWORD

Whatever you can do, or dream you can, begin it.
Boldness has genius and power and magic in it.

—Johann Wolfgang von Goethe

We arrived in San Miguel de Allende, Mexico, on September 11, 2002, along with the bulls who were getting ready to chase Mexicans throughout the center of town for the San Miguelada—similar to the Running of the Bulls in Pamplona, Spain.

"An exhibition of *machismo*," the local paper said. "A chance to flaunt one's manhood before the admiring eyes of their girlfriends." Last year about forty people ended up in the hospital, the paper reports. But the people were excited and having fun—the poor bulls were frightened half to death and running around the plaza nearing exhaustion.

How did we end up being expatriates in Mexico? Michael and I wanted to live in a place for the next several years that was beautiful, interesting, and affordable, with great weather, a community of friends, and opportunities galore. Nothing more, nothing less. After months of research in books and on the Internet, we decided on Mexico. Of course! It was close enough to the United States to be able to come back and visit the kids (although by all indications they would be here before we went back there). Did we speak Spanish? No. Had we been to Mexico before? Just once, on a diving trip many years ago. Did we have friends here? Not a soul. Were we crazy? Perhaps. But there was only one way to find out.

Deep
in
Serenity

Dwayne is an inspiring young chef. One evening, this young black
woman flips his whole world upside down. Serenity, the young
woman, gives him a note, and with that, he has two choices to make.
He can live in the moment and see where that takes him, or he can
choose to stay on course with his normal-ass life. This is a love story
with a typhoon of sexual, erotic adventures of two people taking
chances. Dwayne and Serenity take you on a trip. How long will it last?
How long until they get caught up and life decides to take its turn?

Hello, hello
My name is DaWade Jones, first time writer. Residing in beautiful
Colorado is where I dwell, I enjoy cooking for people and making
new friends. Colorado has been a great place for me, born and
raised in Wyoming. I say the two are almost the same, less wind in
Colorado and the mountains are just as beautiful. The winters here
were a great inspiration writing and helped me with my flow some
mornings, nothing better than going out on the patio when its 40
degrees outside. The snow slowly falling and I can hear the sound of
the snow hitting the cold asphalt.

U.S. $13.99

ISBN 978-1-5320-3088
5139
9 781532 030888

iUniverse®
www.iuniverse.com

ACKNOWLEDGEMENTS

To Michael Gerber, without whose sense of adventure this journey would not have happened. Thank you for your persistence in encouraging me to get this story in print—our travels together are never to be forgotten.

Lulu Torbet came into my life at the perfect time, and with the right blend of talent, humor, and friendship edited this book and calmed my fear of putting it out there. Michael Kleimo, artist extraordinaire, created the cover based simply on a photo of our infamous Subaru minibus. How fortunate I am to have such talented friends living in my little Mexican paradise in San Miguel de Allende.

Finally, to Mary Jo David, who kept all the e-mails I sent her during my travels upon which this book is based—and who still looks forward to reading the finished book! Your enduring friendship makes my world a better place.

Printed in the United States
By Bookmasters